MW00637056

GENERAL MOTORS

STYLI&&&&ARY

They Don't Build Cars Like They Used To!

by Stanley K. Yost

STYLING LIBRARY

Dedication

I dedicate this book to the ever-increasing legion of people who devote countless hours of time and resources to the restoring of early automobiles. Their efforts contribute immeasurably to the preserving of automobile history.

About the book —

This book is not intended to be an all encompassing volume of technical information about the cars discussed. It is a book designed to illustrate, and describe briefly some of the features of early cars that were fantastically impractical, and yet others that were downright ingenious! In some instances, variations of original ideas are still used on modern day vehicles.

"They Don't Build Cars Like They Used To!" — that is true in most cases. Can we say "thank God," or should we say "isn't it a pity." The decision is yours to make as you read the stories, and view the illustrations, of the 94 cars in this book.

One living reminder of the earliest days of the automobile is Mrs. Mary Landon of Elkhart, Ind. She was the office force of the Haynes-Apperson Co. in Kokomo, Ind. at the turn of the century.

In several hours of conversation with Mrs. Landon, she brought forth many interesting and sometimes amusing, experiences of the pioneer automobile manufacturing days.

Many fond memories come to mind as she speaks of men of the automobile world she knew. Such names as the Apperson brothers, Elwood Haynes and John Maxwell turn up as she reminisces. Mrs. Landon was one of the first women drivers — having started in 1898. The amazing fact is that she gave up driving in 1910. Her first experience at the tiller was related in my first book, "The Great Old Cars . . . Where Are They Now?"

9

It was during a conversation with Mrs. Landon in the summer of 1961, that she elucidated the story of the Horsey Horseless Carriage. It was in reality an 1899 Haynes-Apperson.

Some of her memories were relived during that summer, when Mrs. Landon and myself were guests of Mr. and Mrs. Jack A. Frost of Washington, Mich. Also at this address one finds an 1897-1898 Haynes-Apperson. It is beautifully restored, and in perfect running order.

In the photograph supplied by Mr. Frost, I am sure the glow of satisfaction that was reflected in Mrs. Landon's face is evident, as she sits in a Haynes-Apperson sixty-four years later. It was a wonderful reunion between two old friends.

With this spirit in mind, I present the 1899 Haynes-Apperson (Horsey Horeless Carriage) as the first feature of this book.

Stanley K. Yost

Contents

15

A horse's head made this car seem a kin to dobbin!

1899 HAYNES-APPERSON

Use a horse's head — on front of your horseless carriage to prevent a commotion when meeting a horse! This was one answer to the old adage "if you can't beat them, join them." The Haynes-Apperson company gave it a try, but as history records it, they were just "horsing around."

It all started late in 1898 when Uriah Smith of Battle Creek, Mich. presented his idea to the Haynes-Apperson company in Kokomo, Ind. A well stuffed horse's head and neck was to be affixed to the front of a motor-carriage. It was intended to create the image of a horse and buggy, and consequently not disturb the approaching horse.

Elmer Apperson approved of the idea, and in the spring of 1899 the contraption was attached to the front of a new Haynes-Apperson surrey. John Landon (husband of Mrs. Mary Landon) was elected to drive the vehicle into the country to see what Indiana horses thought of Mr. Smith's idea.

Mrs. Landon relates that the experiment was "not satisfactory." Uriah was crushed and returned to Battle Creek. The horse's head remained at the factory for many months, and numerous jokes were made about the venture, but never in front of Mr. Apperson. The great automobile man finally ordered the dummy returned to its creator.

So ended one of the most unusual experiments in the development of the automobile.

Bevel friction drive made motoring easy as A B C!

1909 A. B. C.

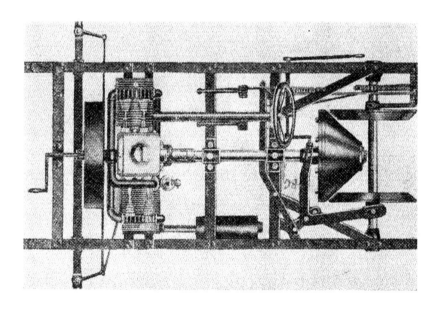

Bevel friction drive — something new for 1909 for the proponents of friction drive from A. B. Cole. Pedals and levers kept the driver busy, and there was no worry about speeding with a 30 m.p.h. maximum!

18

This new patented friction drive was from the A. B. C. Motor vehicle Manufacturing Co. of St. Louis, Mo. Up to this point friction drive had always been a matter of a friction disc with a leather faced contact wheel. The A. B. C. version had a large 16 inch cone and two aluminum and beveled contact wheels.

The bevel wheel nearest the top in the illustration was for forward movement, and the lower wheel for reverse. An outside hand lever controlled the overall speed. It could be adjusted to any position — forward for low speeds, and backward for higher speeds. After the hand lever was moved to the desired position, the bevel wheels were brought into contact with the large cone by use of a foot pedal.

The lower pedal in the illustration facilitated the forward movement, and the opposite pedal controlled the reverse action. A latch arrangement on the forward pedal held it in place for driving at a steady speed for a long distance. Constant pressure was needed on the reverse pedal to make it operate.

The 30 m.p.h. maximum was good for either forward or reverse movement. Reverse could be engaged at anytime, thus making a useful brake.

The Model E shown below was powered by a small cross mounted, two cylinder air cooled engine. A water cooled engine was available for $25 extra. Other additional costs were: pneumatic tires, $75; acetylene head lamps, $25; and cape top, $40. This touring could cost the grand total of $800!

1909 A. B. C.

Passenger comfort was Ackerman's first goal!

1897 ACKERMAN

    Passenger comfort — was a problem to be solved in the gay nineties as well as in the atomic age. Ventilated dash, oversize pneumatic tires and the "Ackerman Spring Wheel" were one man's idea for passenger well-being. From a back yard work shop came the Ackerman—truly a pioneer horseless carriage.

W. K. Ackerman of Detroit, Mich. was not concerned with how to propel his carriage, but how to give it greater riding ease.

He did this with three separate features. A careful look at the close-up illustration reveals the dash to be made of screen wire, which permitted air to pass through. This served the dual purpose of cooling the passenger's feet in addition to supplying a direct current of air to the engine under the seat. The larger than ordinary pneumatic tires were used to absorb the road shock.

The feature attraction of the Ackerman show was the "Ackerman Spring Wheel." All forms of leaf or coil springs had been eliminated. The new arrangement consisted of a wheel hub and steering knuckle that had internal springing.

Although limited in production, the Ackerman was the easiest riding car of the period.

1897 Ackerman

An automobile without a chassis, at $465!

1916 ALSTEL

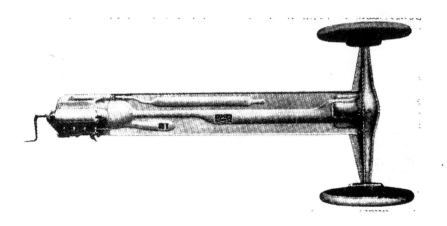

A car without a chassis — unheard of by many car buyers in the period prior to World War I, was a reality in 1916. An electrically welded unit body and three point suspension were two of Alstel's big guns in the automobile sales battle.

Unitized
and how!

The All Steel Motor Car Company of Macon, Mo. bombed the car conscious public with their Charles L. Smith designed 1916 models. The car was road tested for two years before being unveiled as something new and different.

Two rear wheels and a ball and joint socket in the center of the front cross member of the body formed the true three point suspension. Absolute straight line drive was accomplished by eliminating universal joints. The transmission was mounted on the rear axle.

By disconnecting the ball joint, brakes and springs, the entire body could be removed. This was convenient and economical since a new body could be installed for the price of repairing and painting the old one. The same theory applied to the steel wheels. A new wheel cost $3 as compared to $12 for the conventional wood wheel. It was claimed that steel wheels aided tire cooling.

Over all the car was cheaper to operate and buy initially because it had 800 less parts and weighed 750 pounds on a 120 inch wheelbase.

The body was electrically welded. Fenders were welded to the body. This then was an early application of unit body construction. With a price of only $465 one wonders why the Alstel did not survive.

1916 Alstel

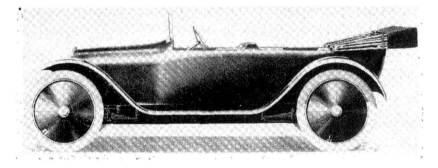

Only five moving parts in this 2-cycle engine!

1909 ATLAS

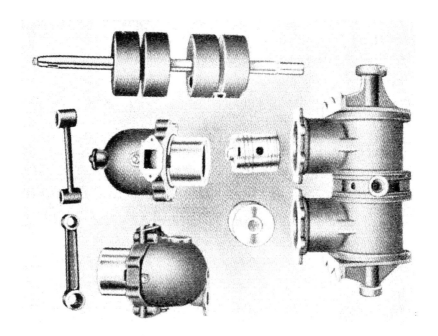

Two cycle, two cylinder engine — with five moving parts that packed a terrific wallop, equal to four cycle offerings for 1909. An impulse every revolution assured smooth performance for this 22 h.p. engine during the era of straight-back fenders and doorless driver's compartments.

The Atlas Co. of Springfield, Mass., under the guidance of Harry A. Knox, produced this successful engine that was to power the company's 1909 automobiles.

There was a two fold problem confronting exponents of the two cycle principle. One was the limitation of speed and power for any given engine, and the other was to create enough speed and power for propelling an automobile.

The Atlas design solved these problems by having high crankcase compression, large multiple inlet and exhaust ports, and a special piston design. The five moving parts were: one crankshaft, two pistons and two connecting rods.

For the buyer who wanted everything, a four cylinder engine was available. Of course this meant a total of nine moving parts to be concerned with.

1909 Atlas Runabout

Diamond wheel arrangement allowed short turning radius!

1907 AUTOCYCLE

"Diamond" wheel arrangement — was another version of how wheels should be located on a car. Two passengers could cycle along at speeds up to 45 m.p.h., and literally turn around on a dime with the Autocycle. This four hundred pound vehicle cost a dollar a pound.

The term "diamond" comes from the fact that there were two wheels in line, as on a bicycle, and two slightly smaller wheels on the sides about a foot away from the tonneau. The drive was on the single rear wheel with power supplied by a six horsepower air cooled engine.

In steering, the front and both side wheels turned. This permitted a very short turning radius. The wheel arrangement idea was practical for driving on the paved city streets of the city of Philadelphia, Pa., where the car was manufactured, but on the rough and rutted rural roads it was a disadvantage.

The unusual Autocycle was manufactured by the Vandergrift Automobile Co. in Philadelphia, Pa.

1907 Autocycle

Motor wheels were first meant for bicycles!

1923 AUTO RED BUG

The motor wheel — primarily a power attachment for bicycles at the beginning in 1919, was eventually converted to use on small buckboards. The driver and passenger rode in bucket seats as they skimmed along over the roads at speeds up to 25 m.p.h.!

Saddled over the twenty-inch diameter motor wheel was a one cylinder, two horsepower gasoline engine. A belt driven fan on the left side cooled the single cylinder. Many different companies manufactured buckboards, among them being the Automotive Electric Service Corp. in North Bergen, N. J., producers of the Auto Red Bug.

The 1923 Auto Red Bug was a two passenger buckboard with wheel type steering. The motor wheel was attached to the rear of the buckboard by a pivot pin. A lever device was provided for the purpose of lifting the motor wheel off the ground when starting the engine, or coming to a halt without stopping the engine.

When ready to start, the motor wheel was lifted from the ground with the lever, and the engine was started much in the same manner as a lawn mower engine. The driver would then take his place behind the steering wheel, throttle the engine down to a low speed, and with the lever, lower the motor wheel to the ground. Speeds from four to twenty-five miles per hour were possible.

The selling price was $187.50, and their popularity extended into the early thirties.

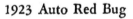

1923 Auto Red Bug

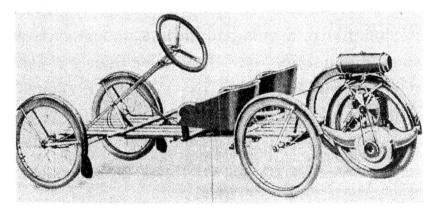

A three cylinder rotary engine for this unit!

1894 BALZER

Three cylinder engine — and a rotary — what an amazing creation for the year 1894! Stephen Balzer developed this mechanical marvel when automobiles were little more than a gleam in a blacksmith's eye. This contrivance rotated vertically around a stationary crankshaft.

This wasn't the only rotary the world has ever known, but it probably was the first. The most famous examples of rotaries were used in airplanes during World War I. These engines rotated in the same direction as the propeller.

The Balzer engine was most like the aircraft types, since it rotated with the propelling factor, the wheels, in this case. The three tin-can-like projections are cylinders. Each contained two valves, one inlet and one exhaust, just like most cars of today.

Fuel passed from a tank under the floor board through a tube to a mixing valve and into a chamber on the rotating crankcase. Tubes in this chamber led to the inlet valves. This same chamber received the exhaust gases and also served as sort of manifold. The incoming fuel was heated and the exhaust was muffled.

Drive was by one rear wheel only, and was accomplished by a short shaft having driving gears and turning with the crankcase. There were three speeds forward, but unfortunately the driver had to get out and push to go backward with this car.

This was the first of several Balzer carriages built in New York City. It was not too unrelated to the gay nineties transportation favorite, the bicycle, with its front wheels and bicycle forks. Total length was barely six feet.

To get a look at the Balzer one must go to the Smithsonian Institution in Washington, D. C.

1894 Balzer

A midget compact car

that almost succeeded!

1930 BANTAM

A midget car — that captured the American youth by storm, but unfortunately the youth of 1930 had not even a small amount of money to buy a small car. Call it Austin Bantam, American Bantam or American Austin, this was one of the most talked about cars in a nation suffering the financial woes of a great depression.

At one time or another this car was called by all three of the aforementioned names, but the 1930 cabin coupe was correctly known as American Austin, the bantam car. Since it was basically English in idea, the title American was prefixed in order to eliminate confusion.

Here was a true midget automobile, not just a light, stripped down car. Initially there were two models: a two passenger cabin coupe, and a two passenger roadster manufactured by the American Austin Co. in Butler, Pa.

Basic specifications pertaining to this distinguished little car were wheelbase, 75 inches; weight, 1200 pounds; horsepower, 7. They combined to make 40 to 50 miles of driving possible with a gallon of gasoline.

Illustrated below is the 1938 roadster which was one of seven available body styles, among them being the four passenger speedster, which was really forerunner of the now famous jeep.

1938 Bantam

This mechanical horse
for two-wheel carriages!

1899 BARROWS

A mechanical horse — which was easy to attach to any regular horse drawn carriage or cart. The horse was on the way out, and C. H. Barrows invented the mechanical horse that he calculated would replace old Dobbin.

The unit consisted of a thirty-six inch diameter wheel with a fork similar to the apparatus used on a bicycle. The bipod framework enabled the unit to be affixed to a regular two-wheel rig. In the case of a four-wheel carriage, the two front wheels had to be removed.

Around the rim of the front wheel, on one side, was a gear track that ran the full circumference of the wheel. At the back, and attached low on the wheel was the power unit. This consisted of a battery or power box saddled on one side, and an electric motor drive spur attached to the opposite side of the front wheel. The motor and spur gear were in line with, and drove the large wheel through the gear track that circumscribed the wheel rim.

Control was by rein, and therefore much like driving a horse. The doctor's carriage illustrated below, was an improved version of the mechanical horse. Protection shields were adapted for the comfort and safety of the passengers. The Barrows was manufactured in Willimantic, Conn.

1899 Barrows

Swivel headlamps permitted seeing around corners!

1904 BEVERLY

Swivel headlamps — as standard equipment on the Beverly, was a giant stride forward toward making night driving more convenient, and practical. Lighting efficiency was increased when the beam was directed to the immediate driving area of the turning car.

Some problems of driving have always been very nearly un-surmountable. Such is the problem of seeing around corners. In 1904 the Upton Machine Co. of Beverly, Mass. tackled this problem with the introduction of their touring car with swivel headlamps.

This is one of the first instances of a car being equipped with swivel headlamps as standard procedure. The shafts on which the headlamps were mounted ran through an opening in the front horns of the frame, and were attached to the running gear.

Here they were connected to the tie rod extending from the steering gear. Upon turning the steering wheel, the headlamps moved in the direction of the turn. Headlamps were therefore more efficient since the light was focused entirely in the path of the turning car. You could see around corners if the $4,000 price of the Beverly touring car did not upset your budget.

1904 Beverly

One headlight for night driving on this car!

1915 BRISCOE

One headlight — permitted middle-of-the road vision during the era of limited night driving. The headlight did not turn with the wheels nor did it have wide spread beams for greater road area coverage. To be on the safe side, extra large cowl lamps were provided for lighting insurance.

Benjamin Briscoe's "one-eyed" car was manufactured in Jackson, Mich. by the Briscoe Motor Co. Publicity stated that the Briscoe was "the first French car at an American price" since it was designed in France several years previously.

The single light was built directly into the radiator shell. When the car made its first appearance you can be sure it invoked much discussion.

The first models sold for $750, but they were minus a generator, self-starter, top, windshield and speedometer. If all these extras were included on the car the price was $900.

After Mr. Briscoe saw the favorable response to his little 1,700 pound car the price was lowered to $785 for a completely equipped touring or roadster.

1915 Briscoe

Coil springs and wood axles gave stamina and comfort!

1910 BRUSH

Deep, heavy coil springs and wood axles — combined with friction joint radius rods and pneumatic tires made the Brush a veritable chariot. Neatness and durability of this car earned the respect of the light car buyer in the duster and goggles era.

What it lacked in size, the Brush made up for in ease of ride and stamina. The body was attached to the under side of the four coil springs at the extreme corners. It was claimed that since the coil springs closed on rebound they were impossible to break.

Axles and frame were made of specially oil treated wood which stopped rotting and checking, and made the wood practically indestructible. Resiliency of wood added to the riding quality.

Alanson P. Brush, adding to his formula of riding comfort and limited car weight, used a one cylinder engine with an unbelievable 7 h.p. kick. Imagine purring along 30 m.p.h. at a fantastically economical rate!

Promoters of the little car from Detroit, Mich. claimed that it was cheaper to own a Brush than a horse.

1910 Brush

Cane finished body panels

by true hand craftsmen!

1931 CADILLAC

Cane decorated body panels — were the ultimate prestige application for the automobile connoisseur. Caning, an art carried over from the quality coach builders of the horse drawn era, was never more beautifully and tastefully applied than on the Cadillac Fleetwood Custom for 1931.

Earliest applications of cane were done as the coach was being constructed. Since cost of labor was negligible in the early days, the amount of time required was accepted without question. As time progressed the caning process had to be speeded up in order to keep pace with more modern construction methods.

First and cheapest speed-up method was to have the cane pattern printed on fabric or paper. This material was cut to fit and pasted on the body, followed by a coat of varnish or lacquer. Needless to say there were many difficulties in applying the fabric or paper to the contours of the body. This necessitated the use of mouldings to cover unsightly joints. Decals were also used to some extent, but failed to give the raised effect associated with a genuine cane finish.

"Art caning" as used on the Cadillac was an expensive procedure, but was good for the life of the car. Cane was laid on the panels in relief, with viscous paint, line after line. Fine guide marks were first put on the body, followed by a special lining apparatus that applied the paint.

The V-16 limousine by Cadillac of Detroit, Mich. was a stock model with a price of $10,000.

1931 Cadillac

A heat operated engine using kerosene or gasoline fuel!

1902 CALORIC

Calorific — meaning the causing of heat. That was the basic idea of the Caloric engine. There were no spark plugs, carburetor or vaporizer, water or fan for cooling, on this engine built by the Chicago Moto-Cycle Co. of Chicago, Ill. It was impossible to overheat this engine!

The Caloric engine could be used as either a gasoline or hot air unit operating on either gasoline or kerosene for fuel. Two cylinders were mounted horizontally, with torches similar to blow torches at the forward ends. Fresh air was taken in at the opposite extremity of the cylinders and compressed by a piston.

Through a separate tube the compressed air was then transferred to the heated cylinder end where it was expanded, thus forcing the piston outward. This process repeated itself as long as heat was maintained on the cylinder.

Gasoline or kerosene was used for fuel to operate the torches, but the gasoline could also be used as fuel in the engine itself. Gasoline passed through coils, and the vapor that was created worked the same as the hot air. There was an impulse every revolution, and the used gas or air was expelled at the return of the piston.

The reason that the engine would not overheat or bind was the fact that the compressed charge acted on a displacement block, rather than a tight fitting piston with rings. This block was more or less floating and would not bind.

1902 Caloric

In 1900 this car had ideas that are still used today!

1900 CAMERON

Advanced — no truer statement could be made of the Cameron from Pawtucket, R. I. The critics said humbug to a front mounted engine under a hood, steering wheel on the left side, and shaft drive. Many years were to pass before other cars utilized the ideas of F. S. Cameron.

The 1900 model was the first effort of Mr. Cameron who was the creator of a car that was later to be seen all over New England. To begin with, the critics condemned the placing of the engine in front of the car under a hood. All the engineering geniuses of the day knew the engine should be placed under the body in the middle of the car. Plus the fact that it was possible to crank the car from the driver's seat, if you had a long arm!

Also at this time, steering customarily was accomplished by tiller or lever. It took courage to introduce the wheel for steering, and of all things, to have it on the left side of the car. The arm chair engineers of the times pointed out that when the driver stopped his car to embark at the curb, he would have to slide across the seat or get out on his side and tramp through the mud.

The shaft drive was an invention of Mr. Cameron's, and with it went his own designed sliding gear transmission and differential. In the case of the Cameron it must be said "They Do Build Cars Like They Used To."

1900 Cameron

Twin engines in one car to eliminate driving worries!

1908 CARTER

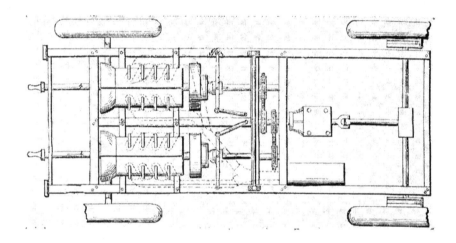

Two engines — was the solution to the problem of engine failure while out on the open road. For rugged going and steep hills just start and operate both engines — fantastic, but true. The home office of the Carter Motor Car Corp. was in Washington, D. C. Perhaps president Theodore Roosevelt appreciated this car since it had power and reliability for the open countryside.

Two engines under one hood must have had its engineering problems. At the beginning it is to be understood that the engines could be run separately, or both together, driving the wheels at the same time. The engines were placed side by side, and except for just a slightly wider hood on the car, it would be hard to tell it from any other car of 1908.

At the rear of each engine there was a cone clutch. Behind the clutches, and attached to the male members of the clutches, were two short intermediate shafts. These extended to a point about half way back on the chassis, where they were joined to a frame cross member. Between these two shafts was another that extended back to the rear axle. This was the drive shaft, and was powered by chains, with conventional transmission and differential being used.

The two four cylinder engines were rated at 24-60 horsepower. Horsepower in this era was rated in various ranges. If it had been a single engine the range would have been 24-30. Speaking of ranges, the price was in the $3,500 range.

1908 Carter

Friction drive was this car's real trademark!

1915 CARTERCAR

Friction drive — meant Cartercar simplicity plus high speed and amazing power. Climb steps if you dared, the demonstrators did; but beware of the local police. It was unlawful, but challenging for the young whipper-snapper who drove a Cartercar!

From beginning to end the Cartercar Co. of Pontiac, Mich. was one of the greatest proponents of the friction drive transmission. Two perpendicular wheels were the main components for Cartercar friction drive.

Power from the engine was transmitted by a rigid shaft direct from the flywheel. Attached to the end of the shaft was a large, flat copper disc that turned the same speed as the engine; thus eliminating any need for a gear box to reduce speed.

The second wheel, looking much like a wagon wheel, was faced with fibre. When the spoked wheel made contact with the revolving copper disc, the axle turned, and consequently the rear wheels were motivated.

One control level was required to make the car move forward or reverse. Push the lever ahead and the spoked wheel moved from the center of the copper disc to its perimeter. Acceleration of the car was controlled by the position of the spoked wheel on the copper disc in relation to the control lever.

As the spoked wheel moved nearer the center of the copper disc, the slower it would revolve. After passing center the wheel would stop, and then turn in reverse. Little wonder the company publicized "Cartercar Simplicity." With this type of power transmission there was no jerking or spinning of wheels.

1915 Cartercar

One foot pedal controlled

acceleration and braking!

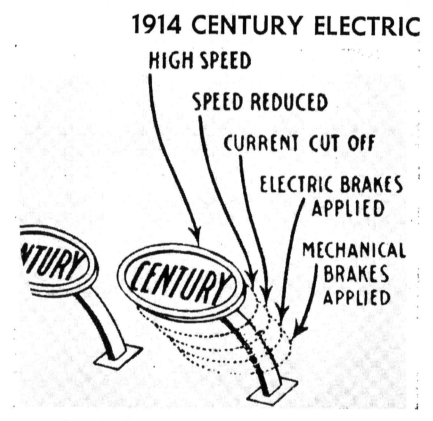

1914 CENTURY ELECTRIC

HIGH SPEED

SPEED REDUCED

CURRENT CUT OFF

ELECTRIC BRAKES
APPLIED

MECHANICAL
BRAKES
APPLIED

Automatic shifts — most generally have been associated with gasoline powered cars. It came as somewhat of a surprise to see an electric vehicle with an automatic shift as a principal selling feature. Electrics were usually thought of as cars with a multitude of different speed variations.

Most electrics had a post control with throttle control operated manually. The Century Electric Car Co. of Detroit, Mich. had other ideas, and the 1914 LB brougham was introduced with the Cutler-Hammer magnetic control. Mechanical specifications were complicated, but the operation was a dream of simplicity. Control was by use of a foot pedal.

The five control positions were in a span of only three inches pedal movement. In conjunction with the automatic control pedal were electric and mechanical brakes. The "non-skidding" electric brakes were designed so that when pressure was applied, it was distributed evenly, thus eliminating skidding or grabbing. In the event of failure of the electric brakes, an auxiliary set of mechanical brakes came into use by pressing harder on the foot control pedal.

The car could be driven either from the front or back seat with use of the master key. The Century with a selling price of $3,250 was priced higher than most other electric powered cars.

1914 Century Electric

This car used gasoline and water as an engine fuel!

1903 CHARTER

Gasoline and water for fuel — half and half to be exact; was the magnificent claim for a car engine invented by James A. Charter from the windy city in Illinois. The idea was not just a breeze, it was actually proven workable. Just imagine filling up with five gallons of gasoline and using water for "mix," in this car from Chicago.

Mr. Charter would be the most popular man in the United States today if he were alive to repeat his amazing development of 1903. Cutting in half the fuel operating cost of almost every gasoline powered engine would be enough to get a man elected to the White House.

The 1903 Charter used water and gasoline that were carried in tanks, and injected into the cylinder heads in atomized form. The gasoline vapor acted in the usual manner, but the water vapor had reactions with completely different characteristics.

When the water vapor reached the heated cylinder it was transformed into super-heated steam. Upon combustion the steam was further converted into hydrogen gas which was then burned with the regular hydrocarbon mixture.

The result was an "explosion that was softer and longer." Combustion was complete, and for the long stroke Charter engine, this type of fuel was ideal.

1903 Charter

Cast steel wheels by Christie for a front drive racer!

1907 CHRISTIE

Cast steel wheels — a design radically different and definitely in keeping with the imagination and spirit of J. Walter Christie. These wheels were a perfect match for the speed and power of the Christie racer.

The name of J. Walter Christie has always been synonymous with front wheel drive, speed and power. It is quite logical that he should design a wheel that was capable of withstanding the terrific stress and strain encountered in racing. These wheels were used primarily on front in conjunction with the front wheel drive.

Spokes and demountable rims were two separate units that made this wheel completely unlike other wheels of note. The hub was cast intregal with the twelve spokes, and the rim bolted to the spokes.

Christie was a great exponent of front wheel drive, and his racers pounded the tracks year after year from 1904. The 1907 racer pictured below (with one wheel missing) had a very large V-4 engine that developed 130 horsepower. Manufacture was by the Direct Action Motor Car Co. of New York, N. Y.

1907 Christie

A car for club members

at discount prices!

1911 CLUB CAR

A club car—not the railroad type, but the exclusive automobile you could purchase at a discount by being a member of the Club Car Company of America. Prerequisites for membership were a high social standing, and of course, some ready money. A "nominal" membership fee was required, but publicity never mentioned how much.

Today we have book clubs, record clubs, travel clubs, dining clubs, and many more clubs that entitle the members to special rates and privileges, all for one thing — money.

Perhaps the earliest of all club ventures was the Club Car Co. of New York, N. Y. The special interest in this story is not the car alone, but the organization and idea behind its inception.

Reasoning behind the club plans was (1) members were to save all showroom expense, (2) to save all selling commissions, (3) to cut excessive advertising costs, (4) to cut racing expenses. The plan was therefore calculated to do away with the extremely high profits netted by the other automobile manufacturers. Savings of up to 35% were guaranteed.

Club members were offered a choice of two models; a seven passenger touring or a roadster. The roadster was not the gentleman's racy type, but a four passenger torpedo styled touring. Both offerings were a product of Merchant and Evans Co. of Philadelphia, Pa., made especially for the Club Car Co.

There was nothing cheap or flimsy about the cars. On a cost plus basis the seven passenger touring sold for $3,000, and the companion car was priced at $200 less. A four cylinder, 50 h.p. engine by the American and British Co. of Bridgeport, Conn. powered the big car. Most of the other popular component names of the day were represented.

A specialty claim of the car was mounting of the engine on a sub-frame which made engine removable possible after loosening only four bolts. While one engine was in for repair, another could be installed immediately, in order to keep you touring in the finest of style. Just another advantage of being a member of the Club Car Company of America — at least for its two year duration.

1911 Club Car

V-3 cylinder steam power car with gas car control!

1922 COATS STEAM

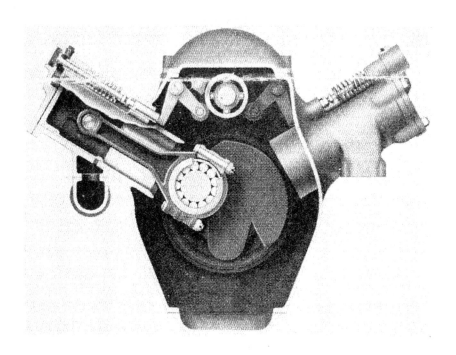

A V-3 cylinder steam engine — in a car that dared to be different at a time when steam cars were nearing the end of their doubtful popularity. The Coats looked like a gasoline car, controlled like a gasoline car, but the V-3 cylinder steam engine was located under the front floor boards!

Several new makes of steam cars were introduced in the early twenties, but the 1922 Coats manufactured by the Coats Steam Car Co. of Columbus, O. was admittedly different. The Coats company must have been believers in the saying, "if you can't beat them, join them," since their car looked and controlled like a gasoline powered car.

To start the engine the driver simply turned a switch, starting a small electric motor which drove a fan and pump. The fan forced air through the fire box, and the pump pressurized the kerosene fuel.

The vaporized kerosene would then be sprayed into the combustion chamber, past a spark plug, which automatically ignited the mixture of air and kerosene. This did away with the pilot light as used in other steam cars.

There were two speeds forward, and one reverse. In most steamers the engine would reverse just by moving a throttle control. On the Coats, reverse was obtained by shifting gears just as done on conventional gasoline powered cars, since the engine turned in only one direction.

This would appear to be a disadvantage as compared to other steam cars of the time, but the Coats company believed the reason that more people did not purchase steam cars was the fact that they were so much different than ordinary cars. They illustrated this point by placing a "clutch pedal" on the floor. This was used only when the driver wanted a burst of steam for emergency acceleration. When the pedal was depressed, steam was admitted to the cylinders for the full length of the stroke.

1922 Coats Steam

Horseshoe front axle made this car low and humpless!

1933 COLEMAN

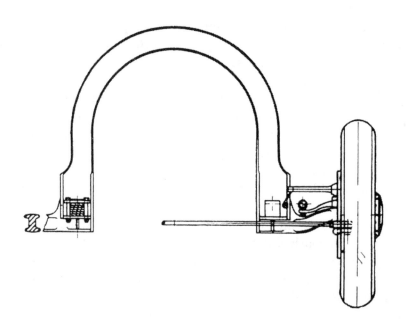

An arched horseshoe front axle with engine mounted within the arch, was the revolutionary idea of Coleman Motors — 1933. The engine thus was four inches lower to the ground, and was positioned farther forward. Advantages: a low, safer gravity center, more passenger space, low hood, greater visibility, more comfortable ride and no drive shaft hump.

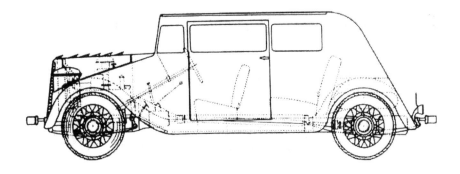

The car was manufactured under the design and patent of H. R. Holmes. There were no fenders as we know the word. On either side of the car the front and rear fender lines and the running board line formed a continuous unit which was deeply flanged. These units were actually the side members of the frame, eliminating all need for a regular frame.

All this was topped off by an economical price of $1,000 for this Littleton, Colo., automobile.

1933 Coleman

Sleeve valve engine cut

parts total by a third!

1912 COLUMBIA-KNIGHT

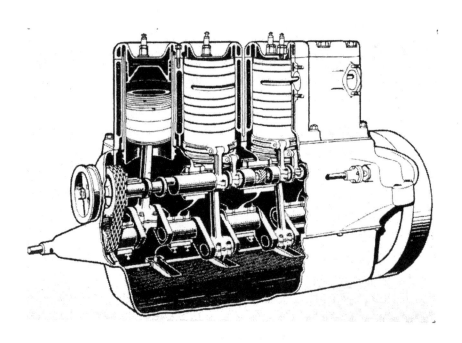

The sleeve valve engine — eliminated the entire system of cam operated push rods, and mushroom or tappet valves. Charles Y. Knight designed the engine in the United States, but it took European manufacturers to prove its merits under actual driving conditions.

To prove his theory, Mr. Knight introduced the new engine in cars of his own make in 1906, but American manufacturers were reluctant to use it at that time. English, German, French and Belgium companies adopted this new engine to their needs. Only after glowing reports of its success reached the United States, did American concerns decide to use the Knight engine.

One of the first to give it a try was the Columbia Motor Car Co. of Hartford, Conn. The main idea of the Knight engine was to eliminate the entire system of cam operated push rods, as well as mushroom or tappet valves. The assembly of front engine gears was done away with, resulting in an overall one-third reduction in number of engine parts.

The cut away drawing shows the two middle cylinders with sleeve valves in place. Each cylinder required two sleeve valves. They were operated by the half time shaft that was turned by the silent chain. The two sleeves moved independently and opposite of each other. When the two slots coincided the sleeve valves were in an open position. At this point the exhaust or intake function took place.

It was a noiseless valve operation that provided twice the valve opening of an ordinary engine. The engine was of standard four cycle type, and the regular suction compression, firing and exhaust strokes followed in succession, the same as in tappet type engines.

1912 Columbia-Knight

Electric magnetic shifting for smooth operation!

1908 COLUMBIA MAGNETIC

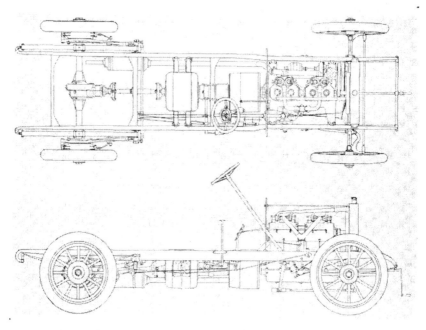

An electric magnetic shift — was to be the answer to all the transmission problems that plagued the automobile manufacturer. Many people were convinced the automobile had been engineered as far as possible! Not so with the Electric Vehicle Co. of Hartford, Conn., which "built a car around the transmission."

The 1908 Columbia-Magnetic had a huge 48 h.p. engine, an electric clutch generator, an electric motor and the usual rear axle, all placed in a conventional manner on the chassis.

When running, the revolutions of the gasoline engine turned the fields of the electric generator which were affixed to the crankshaft. The armature was the end of the drive shaft to the rear wheels.

There was an air space between the generator fields and the armature fields. The revolving generator fields in this way then started pulling the armature around magnetically. This turned the drive shaft and transmitted the power to the rear wheels.

This arrangement necessitated a slight speed differential between the armature and the field, for reasons too technical to explain. The variation caused a slippage never amounting to more than five per cent of the engine speed. Rather than lose this driving force, the designers included the electric motor in the circuit of the generator and mounted it on the drive shaft.

Slippage in a conventionally driven car was lost as heat, but slippage in the Columbia-Magnetic was converted to electrical energy. This current was used by the electric motor to provide full power to the differential.

The gasoline engine could be operated at a rather constant speed, and by moving the controller handle, the speed of the car could be changed. Both the generator and electric motor were said to be capable of withstanding, for a considerable period of time, an overload in excess of the engine power. In this way the transmission became the strongest part of the car.

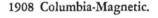
1908 Columbia-Magnetic.

Thermostat heat control
for engine economy!

1920 COLUMBIA SIX

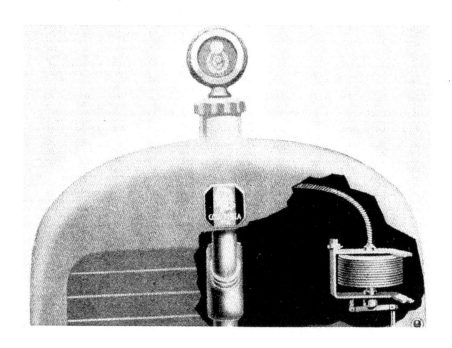

Thermostat control — of engine temperature, induced greater operating economy by reducing excessive heat. An old saying explains, "a watched pot never boils," but no matter how much a driver watched his car's engine, it invariably boiled. The Columbia Six was one of the first cars to employ the Harrison idea for uniform engine temperature.

Many methods were used to retard engine heating previous to the thermostatically controlled radiator shutters. Probably the best remembered method was the use of the winter front. This was an oil cloth or leatherette cover built to fit the entire radiator. It had flaps that could be pinned up or down to regulate the amount of air passing through the radiator.

The Columbia idea was actually a Harrison patent, which used an accordion type thermostat. Water travelled from the upper radiator hose, through a flexible tube and into the thermostat. While the water was still cold, or even at a temperature of 160 degrees, the shutters on the front of the radiator shell remained closed.

As the water temperature increased, this caused the thermostat to expand which in turn moved the rod mechanism down, thus opening the shutters. At 180 degree temperatures the shutters were open all the way, and remained so until the water temperature decreased.

The Columbia Motors Co. of Detroit, Mich. offered their 1920 Columbia Six to the over-heated motorist for $1,845.

1920 Columbia Six

69

A steam carriage featuring all four wheel steering and drive!

1901 COTTA

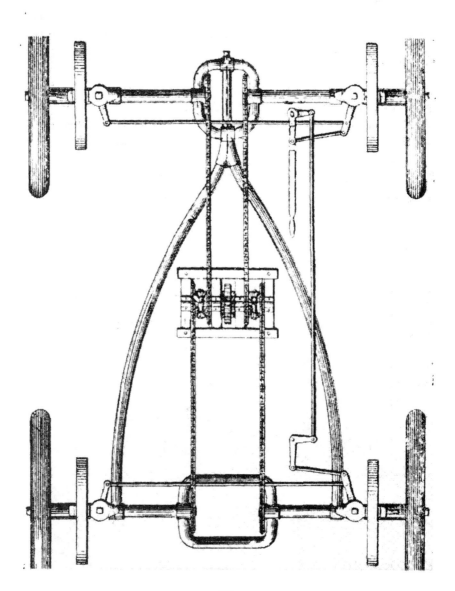

Four wheel steering — and four wheel drive rendered this steam powered carriage completely unlike other cars of the year. Critics viewed with much skepticism the car that started in Lanark Ill. They said it could not be possible, but it was, and it was manufactured for over three years.

The Cotta idea in general was well advanced, and was subject to second guessing in the automobile journals. Steering was by tiller with all four wheels turning on ball joints. The wheels were independent of each other by use of quadruple compensating chain drive. This enabled each wheel to carry an equal amount of the load.

Each of the four short wheel axles was enclosed in a steel tube. Sprockets were affixed to the inside ends of the axles. The two cylinder steam power unit was located in the center of the chassis, with power transmitted by chains to the axle sprockets.

Wheels were attached to the stub axles which were provided with universal joints at the turning points. The wishbone-shaped frame was of an advanced design tubular construction. Selling price of the first Cotta was $850, before the operation was moved to Rockford, Ill.   1901 Cotta

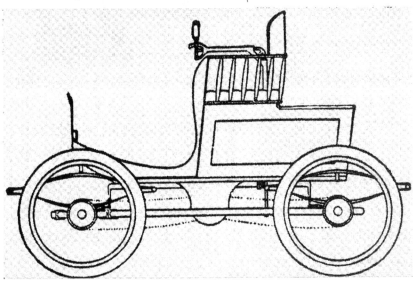

A camping car equipped

for in-car travel living!

1917 CRUISER

Camping car — fully equipped with tent, bed, and all the extras, including hot and cold running water! The comforts of home sprouted from the Cruiser roadster just as World War I nipped it in the bud. First choice went to the army for use as officers' cars.

The Cruiser came on like Gangbusters from several directions at once. Founded in Portland, Maine; offices in Chicago, Ill.; first models built in Indianapolis, Ind.; with aspirations of moving to Madison, Wisc. kept everyone, including customers, in a turmoil.

Most assuredly a fully equipped camping car, the Cruiser had plenty to offer. In addition to the tent and bed for two, there were chairs, refrigerator, stove, fireless cooker, table settings, cooking utensils, hot water tank with plumbing, too, of all things — a toilet tent, and lavatory with hot and cold running water.

Company publicity stated that all these items were stored in or about the car, without obnoxious bulging or unusual body construction. Two very large storage boxes were mounted on each running board. For $1,175 one could have all the comforts of home.

1917 Cruiser

From a touring to pickup truck in one minute!

1911 DAY UTILITY

A utility car — that converted from a touring to a truck with a capacity of 1,000 pounds. Here was one of the finest expressions of an idea that goes back to 1896. Since the Day, there have been numerous attempts to develop a perfect car-truck vehicle.

The magic-like change was accomplished merely by pressing a spring lock, thus enabling removal of the rear seat and doors. Side boards were put in place, and your delivery wagon was ready to go with an 800-1,000 pound load. Farmers and tradesmen, such as plumbers, found this car-truck an ideal unit.

The original selling price of the Day Utility manufactured by the Day Automobile Co. of Detroit, Mich. was $1,150. All equipment to make necessary conversion was included.

The only model variation available was a removable front door and seat. This created a complete wagon type carrier. A rigid wagon seat was available at extra cost.

1910 Day Utility

75

This V-6 air cooled engine weighed only 193 pounds!

1922 DETROIT AIR COOLED

A V-6 air cooled engine — of exceptionally neat design. There were other air cooled engines on the competitive car market for 1921, but none were as completely different as the Detroit Air Cooled. Vibrationless and quiet running, this engine's claim to fame was the low total parts count, and light weight.

As shown in the illustration, construction was of uncomplicated design with all parts easily accessible in time of repair, if needed. The hollow crankshaft of only fourteen inches length, from front to rear main bearing, was designed so as to eliminate all vibrations.

Overhead valves were used, but they were not actuated by rocker arms and push rods as in most other engines. Instead, there was a camshaft housed separately in the trough between the cylinder blocks. All valves were operated by direct-pull rods from this position. This innovation reduced the total number of moving parts considerably.

To combat expansion caused by engine heat, which was a major problem in some of the other air cooled engines, the cylinders were projected down into the crankcase. The noticeable lack of cooling fins was made possible by using very short and thin-walled inlet and exhaust ports. Heat was dissipated rapidly, making additional fins unnecessary.

In keeping with the light weight of the engine, the manufacturers in Detroit, Mich. used an aluminum body. The Detroit Air Cooled was moderately priced at $1,250.

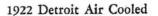

1922 Detroit Air Cooled

Narrow windshield posts

for good driver vision!

1926 DIANA

Narrow windshield posts — permitted a greater range of vision for the driver of the classy Diana. Being able to see in all directions was highly important for the safety operation of a motor car. Some sedans of the twenties had "slabs" for windshield posts that measured up to ten inches wide.

The Diana, manufactured by the Moon Motor Car Co. for the Diana Motors Co. of St. Louis, Mo., had a steel body with all steel windshield corner posts. Use of all steel windshield corner posts made it possible to reduce the posts to a fraction of the size being used on other cars of the year. This was an advance design with a definite aid to driver vision.

Another Diana quality feature of importance was the insulated body. The composite steel body as advertised for the Diana, was built in much the same manner a sound proof wall is constructed. Insulation was built in by the use of coatings and laminations to the body steel.

The Diana was introduced with an eight cylinder engine of lighter construction and lower horsepower than most other engines appearing at this time. The company predicted the popularity of the light eight over the larger, greater horsepower eight cylinder engines.

A near classic, full of spirit, the Diana was ready to travel any road the twenties had to offer.

1926 Diana

Not a transmission or

differential in this car!

1917 DIRECT DRIVE

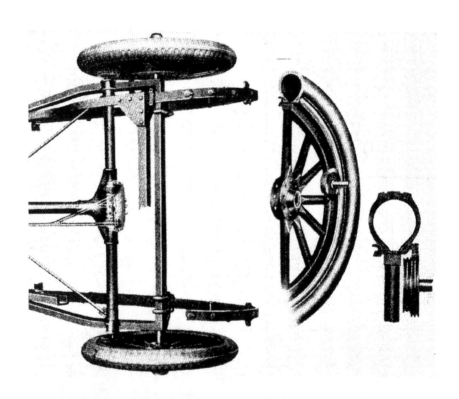

Not a transmission or differential — in the
construction of this car that had engine power
supplied directly to rear wheel rims. Complicated
gear, discs and rear axles were eliminated; resulting in a much more simplified car at a lower cost.

The year 1917 saw the introduction of many unusual and different cars as well as out of the ordinary features. The Direct Drive Motor Co. of Philadelphia, Pa. came up with a real winner in the league of uncommon vehicles, with the unveiling of their 1917 models.

The old style transmission was eliminated, along with all gears, discs, differentials and complicated rear axles. Power was applied directly to rims of the rear wheels. If one wheel became stuck or came off, the power was still transmitted to the other wheel.

The idea is illustrated and shows the drive axles with the rollers on the ends. These rollers engage the V-grooves on the wheel rims, and the power is transferred to the wheels. The rear axle carried the car weight and was a dead axle.

No amount of road jar could affect the drive train. Dirt, dust, and sand had a tendency to increase the efficiency of the drive since friction on the surfaces was greater. The rollers were constructed of high strength steel and were almost indestructible. The drive rings were susceptible to wear, but could easily be replaced for about one dollar.

A single hand lever operated all movements of the control. When driving, a foot lever controlled the speed, started and stopped the car. It was as easy to drive as an electric, and nearly as smooth. There were two forward speeds and one reverse. The drive could be totally disengaged, and the car would coast freely. Prices were reasonable at $700 for the touring and $600 for the roadster.

1917 Direct Drive

Four cylinder, 16 valve
engine of top quality!

1917 DREXEL

Sixteen valves and four cylinders — gave the Drexel engine a superior rating to most six and eight cylinder engines of the day. Simple in construction and low in total number of parts, this power plant was unequalled for acceleration as evidenced by considerable racing success.

The Drexel Motor Car Corp. of Chicago, Ill. was a strong advocate of four cylinder engines. While other companies were producing six and eight cylinder engines, the Drexel organization was devoting its efforts toward four cylinder refinements.

The efficiency of any motor is dependent upon two features more than any other. These are the size of valve opening and the speed of valve closing after intake and exhaust. Using single valves, the size was restricted by the size of the cylinder. If large valves were used, a problem resulted from warping and too much weight. Large valves also required heavy springs which resulted in sluggish performance.

The Drexel four cylinder engine solved these problems by using sixteen valves; two exhaust and two intake valves for each cylinder. The resulting seventy percent increase in valve opening produced instantaneous and snappy acceleration.

1917 Drexel

Rear seat steering wheel

for back seat drivers!

1913 DUCK

A rear seat steering wheel — proved to be one of the most unusual innovations in the annals of car manufacturing. To say it was designed especially for the back seat driver would be an error, but it certainly brings up the question!

The Duck from the Jackson Automobile Co. of Jackson, Mich. was basically a roadster. The illustration shows the car as it looked when outfitted for touring with passengers.

In roadster form the windshield was removed and a cowl fit over the portion where the two front seats were situated. These seats resembled the jump seats used in seven passenger cars. With cowl attached the car looked like it had a hood as long as two thirds the length of the body.

Ladies with big dusters were kept out of the way of the driver's vision when front seat passengers rode along. When touring alone the entire compartment could be used for luggage.

1913 Duck

85

Tilting seat and "self-starter" made this car a stand-out!

1906 DUQUESNE

Tilt the front seat — and at the same time the side door of the tonneau opened to welcome your passengers into the stylish Duquesne. Quality was the byword for the "Dukane" that offered a self-starter and down hill brake to its list of specialties.

The Duquesne Construction Co. of Jamestown, N. Y. was not to be outdone when they introduced their 1906 cars. $2,000 may have sounded high for the five passenger touring, but one must consider the quality.

Convenience of entry by means of tilting the front seat forward, and simultaneous opening of the side tonneau door, was a body construction extra for the owner of the Duquesne.

Slightly more than just turning a key was the self-starter arrangement. It involved stepping on a foot pedal that was attached to the flywheel by a ratchet mechanism, much like a motorcycle starter. A coil spring returned the ratchet to the original position after use.

A second ratchet device held the car when stopped on a hill. Deep teeth were cut into the inside of the rear brake drums; pawls would come in contact with the teeth to hold the car from any down hill movement.

The Duquesne people were very explicit about their name, and spelled it "Dukane" on the nameplate for correct pronunciation.

1906 Duquesne

Do-it-yourself car building kit

for the man who was handy!

1901-02 DYKE

Do-it-yourself — at home in the peace and quiet of your barn or carriage house. Assemble the Dyke car of your choice, and be the proud owner of a horseless carriage; much to the satisfaction of the old gray mare that has pulled your buggy for so many years.

The do-it-yourself craze is not as modern as most people believe. Self-assembled automobile kits appeared on the market as far back as 1899.

Parts displayed on the table were used in constructing the 1900 Dyke from Outfit No. 1. The purchaser had a choice of wheels and tires, depending on type of roads to be traveled. Rural gentlemen would more than likely want the wagon-type wheels with hard rubber tires; while the city dweller probably preferred the wire wheels with pneumatic tires for street travel.

Actual manufacture of the components was by the St. Louis Motor Carriage Co. of St. Louis, Mo. In addition to his car Mr. Dyke operated the St. Louis Automobile and Supply Co. through which he distributed his $700 to $1,000 outfits.

1902 Dyke—Outfit No. 2

Seven cylinder rotary
engine of rare design!

1917 EAGLE-MACOMBER

A rotary engine — with seven cylinders
mounted parallel to the drive shaft was an amazing sight on this sporty car. This unusual engine
weighed only 250 pounds, and developed 50 h.p.
to power this roadster-type car from Sandusky, O.

The Macomber engine was the development of W. G. Macomber, and it was manufactured in several sizes. The small 12 h.p. model was so light that it could be carried by a man under one arm. When placed on a loose mounting and started, the engine ran so smoothly that it did not move from the spot, even at 1500 r.p.m.

The entire principle depends on a revolving angle plate with the connecting rods affixed. The combustion in the cylinder forced the connecting rod back against the angle plate. Since the plate was on an angle it would have a tendency to turn away from the motion of the connecting rod. This resulted in turning of the drive shaft.

With seven cylinders firing, it is easy to understand why the engine operated so smoothly. Fuel reached the engine through the hollow shaft at the bottom of the engine.

The Eagle-Macomber car itself was of the four passenger roadster-type with clean lines and neat appearance. This model sold for less than $1,000.

1917 Eagle-Macomber

The tubular backbone made complete frame rigidity!

1924 FLINT

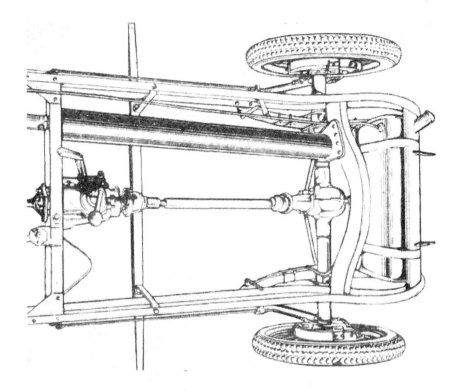

A tubular backbone — constructed from a five-inch tube of steel was a highly publicized selling point for a car that was associated with the famous name of Durant. Frame rigidity was so perfect that a front wheel could be removed, and the car driven without undue difficulty.

Driving on only three wheels was not a practical idea, but it was a method of attracting public interest and attention to the 1924 Flint. The final goal was that of selling cars for the Flint Motor Car Co. of Flint, Mich.

The five-inch tube of steel was riveted through flanges at each end to the second and third cross members of the frame. The tubular backbone forced the cross members to remain in a parallel position, and kept the entire frame in rigid alignment at all times.

This prevented the usual distortion of the frame form road shock, while sparing other working parts from needless wear. A very important benefit, derived from the tubular backbone, was that the rigidity prevented the car body from loosening at the joints.

The leaf springs were utilized to the maximum by absorbing all of the road shock, as they were meant to do. While traveling at high speed the car held the road better, and rounded curves more freely with a reduced turn-over possibility. The tubular backbone was stronger and safer.

1924 Flint

Front wheel drive made power control easy!

1917 FRONTMOBILE

Front wheel drive — could pull your car out of the deepest ruts and over the roughest roads with a minimum of steering calisthenics. Power in front wheels has a natural inclination to make a vehicle travel in a straight line, thereby reducing tendency of skidding, and lost power.

A perfectly engineered front wheel drive system is still a dream to be realized, since the Frontmobile was first offered nearly fifty years ago. C. H. Blomstrom of Detroit, Mich. designed this early front wheel drive effort that was actually produced by the Bateman Manufacturing Co. of Grenloch, N. J.

This front drive assembly required a companion front transmission located at the extreme forward end of the chassis. Placing the engine backward on the chassis provided greater efficiency, resulting from fewer universal joints and connections needed for power transmission to the drive wheels.

The weight from the LeRoi engine and the front assembly was carried on a dead axle. Short drive axles came from the gear box and differential, flexibly mounted on each side of the transmission unit. Universal joints were located at the exits of the gear box, and at the connection of the drive shafts to the front wheels.

An extremely low center of gravity was achieved by a sharp drop in the frame immediately behind the front wheels. Gear shift was mounted on the steering wheel. Controls operated through the steering column. As the salesman once said, "this is the car built on correct principles."

1917 Frontmobile

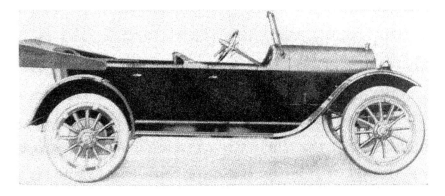

A gearless transmission unit revolved as a flywheel!

1908 GEARLESS

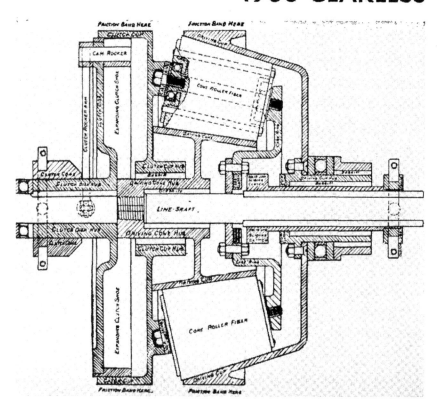

A gearless transmission — designed to harness the seventy-five horsepower engine, gave seventy-five miles per hour speed to the Gearless Greyhound thoroughbred roadster. Here was an ideal car for the daring man who wanted to churn up clouds of dust on a sunny Sunday afternoon.

Understandably, the name "Gearless" has direct bearing on the operation of this car produced by the Gearless Transmission Co. of Rochester, N. Y. The Gearless transmission possessed three distinct drives; one being high speed direct. In this drive the entire mass of the transmission revolved as a flywheel.

Low forward speed was by frictional engagement of five large fiber, cone shaped rolls. They revolved on, and in, an exterior and interior cone. These two cones co-acted with a sliding, double-faced solid jaw clutch which was moved to the forward extreme to obtain low speed drive. Movement of the clutch to the rear resulted in reverse drive.

The internal cone was constantly spring pressed toward the external cone so there was always enough friction to make the five cone rollers revolve without slipping. The entire arrangement required two exterior friction bands, but the same speed and direction changes were obtained as in the common planetary transmission.

There were no toothed gears in the entire unit. This resulted in silent operation and any change was possible under all conditions.

1908 Gearless

A traction drum propelled this early Illinois car!

1902 GLOVER

A traction drum — energized by a chain drive and four cylinder engine, was the driving force for this pioneer car. The drum had two side discs with face plates of soft cast steel bolted between, that came in contact with the road surfaces.

This tiller guided car was built by George T. Glover in Chicago, Ill. It was literally a five wheel car, and when tested proved to be efficient. Power was transmitted from a front mounted four cylinder horizontal engine to the large traction drum by means of a gear and chain drive. The drum was located in the center of the car, and came in contact with the road under spring tension. The car could be raised at least six inches with the drum still making contact.

The drum had two side discs with face plates of soft steel bolted between. The steel discs normally made contact on the road under the weight of the car and the added spring tension. The center plates were readily removable, and could be replaced with toothed plates for use in snow or ice for winter driving.

When the car was operated on sand or mud, the drive came through the face plates. This accounts for the tractor-like tread as shown in the illustration. Countershaft and chain were used in most cases, but a gear transmission was available.

The drum was twenty-six inches in diameter and had a ten inch face. In 1903 a test was made to point out the car's pulling power. The car pulled two heavy coal wagons, weighing two tons each without a load. The wheels of one wagon were locked so they would slide. It was necessary to put two men on the rear of the car to keep it from lifting off the ground!

1902 Glover

The new skirted fenders
created fresh designs!

1932 GRAHAM

Skirted fenders — produced a silent revolution that was to rock the automobile style world for many years. Up to this point, the shell fender design had been accepted by manufacturers and car buyers as satisfactory. The skirted fender ended all this, and public acceptance of the new style was overwhelming.

From the first introduction of skirted fenders on the 1932 Graham by the Graham-Paige Motor Corp. of Detroit, Mich., the new style captured the imagination of almost everyone. If the Graham-Paige organization had done nothing else in their history, the new fender style would have been enough to make them remembered. Skirted fender styling was adopted, and used by many manufacturers for a number of years.

The Graham featured outboard springs, rubber mounted engine, and self-equalizing brakes. Shock absorber reaction was controlled by a knob on the dash, as was the free wheeling device.

Selling price of the rumble seat model was approximately $1,000. The exciting design was to live for many years in the form of a complete line of miniature automobile toys, manufactured by a company in Chicago.

1932 Graham

The cow catcher front end
on a "road locomotive"

1903 GROUT STEAM

A cow catcher front end — on a steamer during the era of the car nickname "road locomotive." In reality the odd shape of the front end was part of the condenser unit that rendered seventy-five per cent of the exhaust steam reusable.

At one time the automobile was referred to as a "road locomotive." The Grout Brothers of Orange, Mass. must have taken the term to heart on their 1903 tonneau. Beside being the first steam tonneau ever shown, it was most likely the first one with a cow catcher front end.

The cow catcher was actually part of the condenser which was placed slightly behind. Through this patented condenser seventy-five per cent of the exhaust steam was reused. This enabled the car to travel greater distances on one fill of water.

Grout Brothers specially designed pilot light needed no spirits or irons to ignite. An ordinary match did the job. With the pilot light it was possible to keep up a full head of steam for periods of two hours, without the loss of a great amount of gasoline or kerosene, and little loss of water.

The pilot light alone could maintain pressure. There was a positive guarantee against the fire being blown out under any circumstances. With the Grout pilot light there was no lighting back, no tube for fuel passing through the boiler, and a cent and a half per mile driving cost was possible.

Another of the Grout patents was the air scoop located on top of the hood. This was a down draft scoop that forced all combustion fumes down, and to the rear of the car. The "Grand Tonneau" model also had ease of control. The driving speed was controlled by a second steering wheel as shown in the illustration. It worked on a ratchet, and had nine different speed positions.

1903 Grout Steam

The horizontal flywheel was a gyroscope to steady this car!

1908 GYROSCOPE

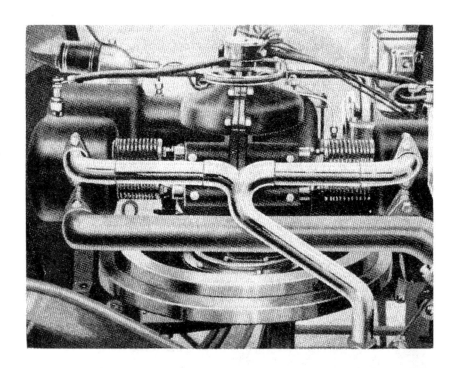

A gyroscope — puts up resistance, as it spins, to any change of direction in the axis of its rotation. In a car this meant absorbing road shock and resistance to overturning and skidding, while cornering at high speeds.

The gyroscope principle was used in a car built in 1906. C. H. Blomstrom, an inventor in his own right, saw the potential of this idea, and purchased the basic patents. The illustration shows the engine of the 1908 Gyroscope car as used by the Blomstrom Manufacturing Co. of Detroit, Mich.

The large flywheel placed on a horizontal plane, did as all other gyroscopes had done; it resisted all shocks of the road and kept the body on an even keel. In taking a corner at high speeds the rotating flywheel had a tendency to resist the overturning effort of the car's inertia. Steering was aided, due to lessened resistance to the change of direction on the same plane.

The Gyroscope runabout was powered by an eighteen horse power engine and sold for $750.

1908 Gyroscope

This rumble seat was a style trend preview!

1918 HAL TWELVE

The rumble seat — a style most generally associated with the roaring twenties, was previewed in the 1918 Hal Twelve. Little did anyone realize that the rumble seat was to become a favorite with the young-at-heart driving set.

To most people the rumble seat has always been associated with the hip flask, and rolled stockings of the twenties. The Hal Motor Car Co. of Cleveland, O. pre-dated this trend with the introduction of their 1918 Hal Twelve, model 25.

For a true picture of the rumble seat, disregard the top, since it was only a bad weather emergency measure. The Hal rumble seat was a very neat arrangement, and folded completely into the rear deck.

The arm brackets slid forward and down, taking the arms with them, so they were below the level of the rear deck when folded. The back of the seat folded forward and down to make a water tight seal, with an unbroken appearance line of the rear deck.

In keeping with the sporty rumble seat, the Hal Twelve was available in almost any color. It required 3,750 pieces of that all important green paper to own this car.

1918 Hal Twelve

Two axle systems on this
front drive, non-skid car!
1930 HAMLIN

HAMLIN PATENTED FRONT WHEEL DRIVE
FRONT WHEEL BRAKES REMOVED TO SHOW DRIVING MECHANISM

Rear Axle

Two axle systems — permitted all weight to be carried on a dead axle. The low placement of axles made possible an extremely low center of gravity for a road hugging silhouette that was becoming popular in the thirties. Coupled with front wheel drive, this car was advertised as one that pulls instead of pushes.

The Hamlin Motor Co. of Chicago and Harvey, Ill. was the oldest and loudest proponents of front wheel drive in the United States when they introduced their car for 1930. It was called the front drive, non-skid car. The Hamlin patents differed somewhat from other front wheel cars of the times.

The wheels turned on huge ball joint universal housings. The car was noted for its remarkably short turning radius. A two axle system left all of the weight carrying to a dead axle. Notice the low placement of the dead axle and also the rear axle. This permitted low body construction which was getting to be an important item in this automotive period.

The full floating drive axles were encased in housings and were completely protected. The front drive and axle illustration is minus the front wheel brakes for sake of description.

1930 Hamlin

Reverse engine rotation by changing position of cams!

1906 HARRISON

A reversible engine — from a builder of wagons! Amazing, but true, this was just one of the Harrison tricks for 1906. A down hill air braking system was incorporated into the engine to economize on fuel and conventional braking.

The Harrison Wagon Company of Grand Rapids, Mich. was the builder of wagons superlative. Craftsmanship was of the highest mark, and their 1906 automobile was no exception.

The reversible engine was made possible by using opposed side cams. One cam was fixed to the cam shaft while the other was movable. They were adjustable to two different positions. If the cams were turned one way, the motor was reversed without changing the firing order. Move them gradually in the opposite direction and the motor would come to a stop before reversing.

This is very unusual, and except for a few in automotive history that have revolved in reverse while running normally, most engines have turned clockwise. Adding to the unusualness of this engine was the self starting procedure. Just pull a knob on the steering post, and it is assumed that compressed air did the work.

The air braking feature was quite different for cars of this vintage. A hand operated air valve opened into a cylinder supply line. The line had feeders to each cylinder, and as the valve was opened, pure air was released into the cylinders. At a corresponding time the fuel mixture was discontinued.

As the air was compressed in the cylinders it formed a substantial cushion. The idea was to utilize the engine for down hill braking, and also conserve fuel and minimize the strain on the regular braking system.

1906 Harrison

111

A giant closed car selling for a big $25,000 price!

1921 HEINE-VELOX

A giant size car — that may well be called the largest production car manufactured in the United States. Engineers at the Heine-Velox Engineering Co. of San Francisco, Calif. must have worked overtime to design this huge, and yet advanced car. A view of the front interior reveals the massiveness that was characteristic of the car from the Golden Gate city.

This great car was actually manufactured and tested a full year before introduction in 1921. Much of the equipment used could be classified as firsts for the industry. For instance, the use of hydraulic brakes on all four wheels, and windows mounted in rubber mouldings, were features well advanced for the model year. The no-glare, extreme slope windshield, was a style soon to be copied by other manufacturers.

The area where the spring horns protruded in the front and rear of the car, was neatly finished and made into storage compartments. There were locked compartments on both running boards for additional storage space.

An unusual construction idea was used in mounting the body to the chassis: In most cars of the day the body was placed on top of the chassis. The Heine-Velox body was placed down over the chassis, with the sides of the body on the outside of the frame members. An important result was a low-slung appearance, and low center of gravity. The floor was below the level of the frame member, producing somewhat of a step-down design. Flooring was also a portion of the cross member design, and made for exceptional rigidity.

Radiator placement was directly behind the front axle line. This prevented radiator damage caused by front axle torsion and frame strain. A twelve cylinder engine was used to power this 4,500 pound machine with a 148-inch wheelbase.

1921 Heine-Velox

V-8 engine with each cylinder cast singly and aluminum pan!

1907 HEWITT

V-8 power — the Hewitt from New York, N. Y. had it in 1907. There have been all types of engines used to supply power for cars of the past and present. The most glorified and highly publicized engines have been the V-8's. They are not new, since one of the first V-8 engines was created for the Hewitt.

The Hewitt engine had cylinders placed at a 90-degree angle, with an aluminum crankcase. Water jackets and cylinder heads were cast intregal, with each cylinder attached separately. All sixteen valves operated from a single camshaft.

The cooling system was a work of art. Cooling water entered each cylinder through an individual water pipe at the bottom of the cylinder jacket. The water as it was warmed, passed up and around each cylinder and valve chamber, coming out at the highest point. Water returned by separate tubes to a central pipe where it returned to the radiator. With this type of system all possibilities of steam or water packeting were eliminated.

The exhaust system was quite unique for the times. Small exhaust manifolds extended upward from each cylinder into the large manifolds, one for each side. The exhaust gases then passed to the mufflers at the rear of the car.

Being one of the first V-8's to appear on the American car market, most of the engine components had to be made from original designs. The same was true of the electrical and carburetor system which were created specifically for the eight cylinder engine.

There were few cars larger than the Hewitt, and the price was also large — $4,500.

1907 Hewitt

Why have six cylinders when five will work!

1907 HEYMAN

A five cylinder engine — that proved the point that cylinders need not come in even numbers to make an engine workable. The Heyman was the most unique car to be shown at the Boston automobile show in 1907. Under the barrel hood was another barrel that contained the group of cylinders.

The five cylinders were nested together with all the axis parallel. The nest of cylinders was surrounded by a brass casing which could be called a water jacket. As partially shown in the illustration, this gave a drum or barrel appearance to the engine.

The cylinders were each 4½ by 5, and the method of operation, while difficult to explain in writing, would not be hard to understand if seen in person. All of the pistons acted on a disc, the center of which was pierced by the engine shaft, or crankshaft. The crankshaft was slightly off true center, and transmitted a wobbling or eccentric motion to the disc. At the true center of the disc was a long pin which was pivoted on the engine shaft by a crank arrangement.

When the pistons acted on the disc, then the disc was forced to turn, and consequently turned the shaft, and eventually the drive train. Alternate cylinders fired in sequence, and five impulses took place every two revolutions of the crankshaft.

Manufactured in Boston, Mass. by Edward Heyman, the 1907 Heyman came equipped with eccentric triple roller clutch type transmissions with any number of available speeds. $4,000 was the price for this car with the barrel hood and barrel-shaped engine.

1907 Heyman

Wheel hub motors moved this carriage at 15 m.p.h.!

1899 HUB ELECTRIC

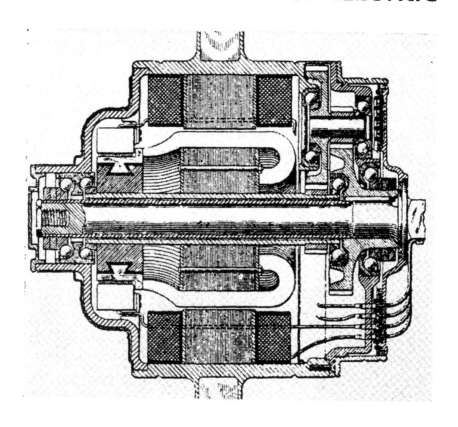

Motors in the wheel hubs — made this carriage one of the most unusual and dependable vehicles in the early electric era. Set your speed at four, seven or fifteen miles per hour and you were sure to arrive on time.

The armature was built on a tubular sleeve which surrounded the axle, and the fields were constructed in the hub shell. The fields rotated with the hubs.

The same principle exists today in the working of a modern electric appliance that has a motor shaft. In the case of the Hub, the motor shaft was in reality the axle of the carriage. Wheel hubs were eleven inches in diameter as compared to the huge forty-two inch wheels.

The Hub Electric was a product of the Hub Motor Co. of Chicago, Ill., with actual construction done by the Westinghouse Co. in Pennsylvania. The elegant carriage was the design of Joseph Ledwinka.

1899 Hub Electric

Spring steel wheel spokes and tires of leather!

1915 INGRAM-HATCH

Spring steel wheel spokes — were the most publicized feature of the revolutionary Ingram-Hatch. Each spoke acted as a spring. Compressed air cushions between the spokes were designed to help absorb road shock. The leather and steel tires were puncture proof.

The Ingram-Hatch Motor Corp. of Staten Island, N. Y. manufactured this car that had a host of unusual features, the most publicized of which was the Ingram wheel. The wheel spokes were made of sections of vanadium spring steel. Each spoke was carefully tempered, and placed so that each acted as a spring.

A series of fourteen heart shaped spokes, located seven on each side of the hub, made up the Ingram wheel. Compressed air cushions were placed between each spoke. All impact to the wheel was equally distributed around the circumference.

Tires were made of sections of leather filled with a resilient substance. These tires were puncture proof, and were said to outwear rubber tires of the day. Each tire section could be replaced individually.

Besides the unconventional wheels, the car was equipped with an air cooled, four cylinder engine that operated on kerosene. It also had a double friction drive. A single short shaft went from the engine to a point midway on the chassis. At this point there were double gears with two drive shafts coming out toward the rear. The friction discs were placed on the ends of these shafts, and the drive discs were attached to the rear axle.

With these many features this could be called the "no" car. It had no gasoline for fuel, no clutch, no radiator, no magneto, no gear shift, no water system, no fan, no carburetor, no water jackets, no timers or selective transmission.

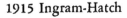

1915 Ingram-Hatch

Two crankshafts for one engine defied tradition!

1904 INTREPID

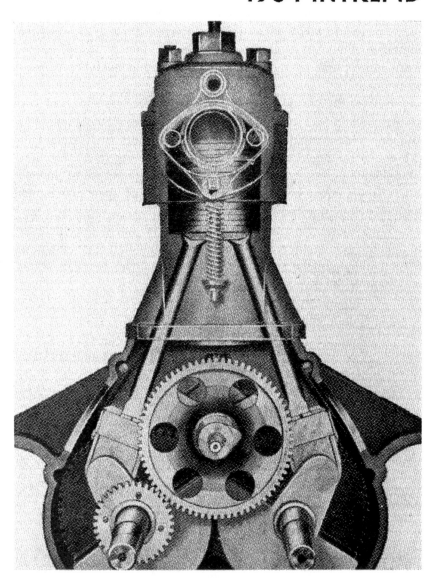

Two crankshafts — rendered the engine completely vibrationless, and entirely different from other engines of 1904. The company specialized in boat engines, but they got into the automobile swim with their eight horsepower roadster.

Two cylinders and one crankshaft was the accepted theory for engine construction of the day. Not so for the Rotary Motor Vehicle Co. Boston, Mass., who changed the tradition. They got their one's and two's crossed, and produced a ONE cylinder engine with TWO crankshafts!

The crankshafts were contra-rotating, weighted, and each had a piston rod. Base of the piston had two connections and both rods were attached to individual crankshafts. The drive shaft operated from one rotating centrally located shaft, turned by the crankshafts. Perfect synchronization was necessary in order to produce smooth easy power.

1904 Intrepid

Cat eye headlights offered night driving safety!

1930 JORDAN

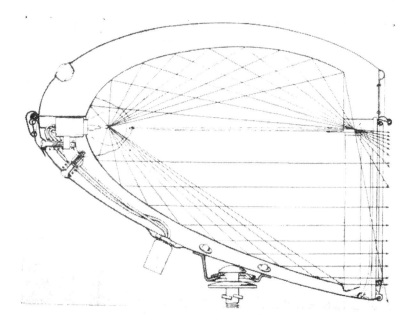

Cat eye headlights — officially called Woodlites, appeared on many cars in 1930, but no application was more distinctive or beautiful, than on the Jordan. Insufficient light, and unbearable glare were two night driving problems that induced the creation of an improved headlight.

The Woodlite Co. of California recognized the need for an improved headlight, and painstakingly designed a headlight that they believed would improve night driving. Two paramount causes of night driving accidents were inadequate light and extreme glare when approaching oncoming cars.

The first deviations from conventional headlight design were to eliminate the parabolic reflector, and alter the position of the bulb. The location of the bulb was the most noteworthy change in design.

Notice that the bulb center is level with the front opening in the lens. This confined the upward glare to an absolute minimum, and concentrated the light beam below the windshield line of oncoming cars. The light beam was also reflected to the side of the road for improved visibility.

Woodlites were in direct contrast to the huge ten or twelve inch headlights with protruding lenses that had been used on cars previously. The Jordan Co. of Cleveland, O. was quick to sense the importance of the Woodlites, not only for their lighting potential, but for the lift they gave in appearance to the $5,500 Jordan roadster.

1930 Jordan

Cantilever springs made
for riding comfort!

1912 KING

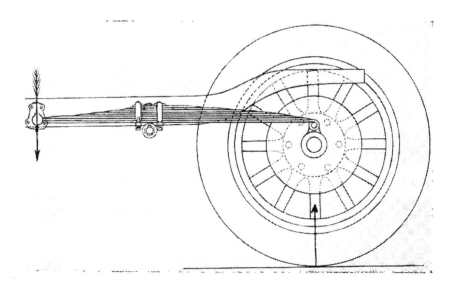

Cantilever springs — as designed by Charles B. King were first used on the car bearing his name in 1912. This was an attempt to spare car passengers of the earthquake-like shocks resulting from travel on the early unimproved roads. Versions of this suspension system were to appear on many cars in the years to follow.

One of the greatest strides forward ever taken in car suspension, was made by the King Motor Co. of Detroit, Mich. on their 1912 models. The King Patented Spring Suspension was new to the automobile field and appeared later on many cars as the cantilever spring.

The King spring was long and flat with more spring behind the pivot than in front. The pivot and front point of the spring were firmly attached to the car frame. The rear end of the spring was in a shackle mounted on the rear axle housing.

With this spring there was absolutely no side sway. Thus road holding characteristics were greatly enhanced. As indicated in the illustration, the road shocks were taken by the wheel and the lever action of the spring, and then directed downward again. No auxiliary shock absorbers were used on the King and it still was one of the easiest riding of all cars.

Special mention must be made of the extreme slope of the windshield. Such an angle is generally associated with cars of the late thirties. Also of unusual interest is the deep-dish style steering wheel, which only recently was revived as a completely new safety feature for drivers.

1912 King

The all-year body turned
a touring into a sedan!

1916 KISSEL

All-year body — that made two cars out of one. A touring for fresh air summer driving; a cozy sedan for chill winter motoring were yours by simply changing tops. Tourings were on the way out, but not before the invention of the all-year bodies.

Automobile manufacturers experienced a great upheaval with the creation of the all-year body. Kissel first used it in 1915, applied for a patent in 1917, and by the time a patent was awarded it was 1922, and the day of the convertible automobile was over.

Nevertheless the all-year body was a useful idea, and it spanned the transition from the touring car to the true closed car. It was the product of two great minds, W. L. Kissel and J. F. Werner of the Kissel Co., Hartford, Wisc.

As shown in the 1916 touring illustration the entire top was removable. This necessitated storage space, but you were really acquiring two automobiles for the price of one. Several clamps held the sedan top in place after lowering it on the body.

Illustrated below is the 1917 four passenger sedan, and the same car as it would look with the summer top. Prices totaled between $1,450 and $1,885.

1917 Kissel

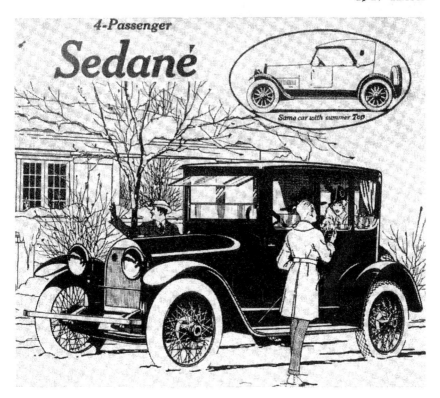

Daring pull-out drawer seats

to carry extra passengers!

1920 KISSEL

Pull-out drawer seats — that gave a new dimension to the passenger carrying ability of sporty roadsters. Climb aboard, and zip along at sixty miles per hour, with nothing more than the driver's collar to hold on to! Here was an innovation on a car that denoted speed, individuality, and true motoring excitement.

The Kissel Motor Car Co. of Hartford, Wisc. was among the first to realize that no matter how beautiful a two passenger roadster may be, it still had limited appeal since it could only accommodate two people. Their solution to the problem was that of adding auxiliary seats. Not ordinary seats, but folding, store away, drawer type seats.

The drawers were located just ahead of the rear fender, one on each side of the car. The mechanics of the drawer seat patent were not complicated, and on earlier models there was much less detail. Just unlock the drawer, reach under the recessed area, and pull out the drawer. Built-in stops were used to keep the drawer from extending too far or tipping with a seated passenger.

Arm rests were wrapped in leather and folded into the seat cushion. The back rest folded on top of the arm rest and seat cushion. When neatly folded, the compact seat was easy to slide back into the body proper. The sliding mechanism consisted of two rails mounted under the seat portion. The rails were positioned in such a way, that when both seats were pushed into the body they had ample clearance.

To make riding in the drawer seat less precarious, nickel plated foot braces were fastened to the running boards. Traveling long distances under such conditions was not encouraged, but the problem of accommodating extra passengers had been solved.

1920 Kissel

Water cooled brakes stopped this car in complete safety!

1907 LOZIER

Water cooled brakes — on this huge $5,000 touring from Plattsburg, N. Y. eliminated brake fade out or failure. Constant pressure could be applied for long periods of time without damaging the brakes. The Lozier was a fast, powerful car, and this brake system was a perfect safety companion.

The brakes were the internal contracting type on the jack shaft, near the driving sprockets. Brake bands were faced with brass and acted on cast steel drums. The drums were specially channeled to carry the water that was delivered to them from a supply tank. Water was under air pressure and was released by control of the driver.

Another feature of the Lozier brakes were the rods from the brake pedal to the levers in the rear. These were fitted with interposed coil springs which equalized the pull on both brakes. It was impossible to lock the brakes, or even worse, lock one brake; resulting in a sprung jack shaft. With the water cooled innovation, and the equalizer springs, brakes could be used for long periods of time without ruination.

Also shown in the illustration is the back-stop device. This was a ratchet-toothed wheel with a pawl that was thrown into contact by a lever on the change gear quadrant. When engaged, the car could not roll back down a hill. This was a very useful idea in case of engine failure or just ordinary parking on a steep grade.

1907 Lozier

Worm gear drive power transfer was efficient!

1915 LYONS-KNIGHT

Worm gear drive — reduced the unsightly differential hump, gave longer life, and permitted smoother transmission of power to the rear wheels. At low speeds there was no annoying jerking caused by loose fitting gears.

The worm gear at the end of the drive shaft entered the differential housing on the bottom side. A smaller type ring gear was used, thus allowing for a smaller housing, which in turn required much less clearance.

The Lyons-Knight from the Lyons-Atlas Co. of Indianapolis, Ind. was one of the first American cars to feature worm gear drive. It was publicized that this new idea would make differential gears last longer, operate smoother and cause less trouble. Since the spiral parts of the worm gear were in direct contact at all times with the ring gear, there was no looseness or play between gear teeth.

With no looseness in the gears, jerking and bucking while driving at low speeds were eliminated. The illustration shows the open gear case and the worm gear. The inset indicates the gear that the worm drives, and the axle shafts come out where the roller bearings are located.

With much less housing clearance required, the body of the car was lowered considerably. Worm gear drive was more expensive than other units, but the Lyons-Knight offered the car owner a little more quality for his money. The seven passenger limousine was a plush car selling for $4,300.

1915 Lyons-Knight

The plush interiors were
this car's claim to fame!

1917 MAJESTIC

Fabulous outfitting — that challenged all companies to put "touring" back in the touring car. Everything from a cigar lighter to an ice box makes this car a perfect example of "they don't build 'em like they used to!"

The Majestic Motor Co. of New York, N. Y. brought their car to the attention of the public by emphasizing its touring capabilities. From the special two bulb headlamps to the softly rounded Victoria top, the Majestic was a car of luxury. Attractiveness was more than skin deep, there being a V-8 engine under the hood.

Only the highest grade leather was used for upholstery. Extra thick carpeting with a waterproof oil cloth backing enabled the driver to preserve the carpet by turning the waterproof side up during a rain. Material for the Victoria top was of the finest, and the inside was padded.

The back of the front seat was paneled in mahogany with compartments built in. The center section was really a folding table. The door could be raised up on hinges to form the table for a entire group to eat their lunch in the car. On the shelving in the section was room for lunch boxes, touring equipment.

To the right of this compartment was another that held a custom built thermos and cigar lighter. To the left was a similar compartment containing custom built solid food containers, and a small vacuum ice box.

Another handy item in the tonneau was a lady's toilet set with mirrors included. To top off the luxurious appointments were the nickel plated full length robe bar and the padded full length foot rest. Everything was for passenger comfort. All for $1,650.

1917 Majestic

Rear mounted transmission was different for 1907!

1907 MARION

A rear mounted transmission — made possible the elimination of the sub-frames, chain drives, jack shafts, supporting rods and other paraphernalia that cluttered the undercarriage of other automobiles. The Hassler transmission was simple and light weight, but it permitted a nearly straight drive shaft, and minimized power loss.

Imagine the impact this car had on people who were used to seeing the complicated undercarriage, to say nothing of the huge bulky transmissions, and the big dust pan that covered the underside of the motor and transmission. The massive low-slung appearance was in direct contrast to the trim little Marion.

Robert Hassler was the genius behind the transmission that appeared on the 1907 Marion from Indianapolis, Ind. It was a new type sliding gear transmission that mounted on the upper part of the rear axle. This resulted in a nearly straight drive shaft that cut power loss considerably, since only one universal joint was needed.

The neat and simple Marion tourabout rig was speedy and desirable to own. You received a 24 h.p. engine and 1600 pounds of automobile for $1.25 per pound!

1907 Marion

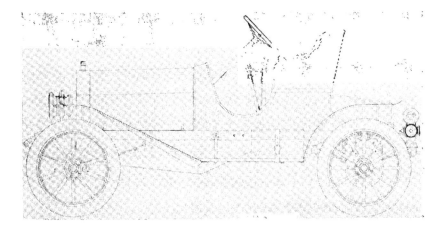

A V-four engine and double 3-point frame suspension!

1905 MARMON

A V-four engine — and double three-point suspension was the Marmon platform to the goggle-eyed motorist of 1905. An air cooled engine powered the car that "rides like a sail boat." This mechanical masterpiece was a prolific seller during the duster and veil era.

The Nordyke and Marmon Co. of Indianapolis, Ind. created this popular early automobile that was to be long remembered for its double frame construction.

The main frame supported the body and passengers, while the sub-frame carried the engine, gear train and rear axle. Made of pressed steel filled with wood, the sub-frame was mounted on trunnions to the front springs, and rocked on the differential case and rear axle. The main structure, mounted with trunnions on the rear springs, and rocked on extensions of the sub-frame in front. Driving strain was alleviated with torsion bars going from the axles to side members of the frame.

A favorite demonstration stunt of the Marmon company was to jack a front wheel one foot off the ground and then raise the opposite rear wheel the same height. The remaining two wheels would stay firm on the ground while the body maintained an almost level position. The "sail boat ride" was a Marmon claim.

Under the bonnet of this typical looking (for the period) car, was one of the first V-four engines. The cylinders were set at a 45 degree angle to permit a shorter bonnet and to induce better air circulation.

All of the mechanism was placed on the top sides of the cylinders for easy servicing. Valves operated by long push rods and walking beam levers, with exhaust ports located at the bottom of the cylinders.

1905 Marmon

Adjustable steer wheel for entering and driving ease!

1904 MARR

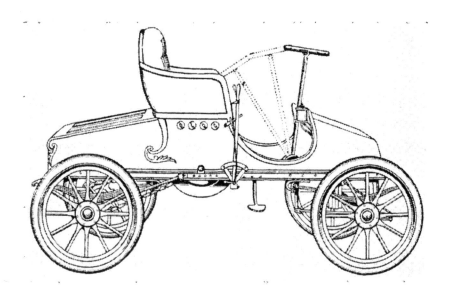

Adjustable steering wheel — for the portly man or the woman with the stylish, bulky skirt of 1904. The Marr swing away steering wheel could be set forward or back in many positions, as desired to accommodate varying waistlines. No need to cut calories, just move the wheel!

Ease of entrance into the automobile was "solved" in 1904 by Walter L. Marr when he introduced his version of the adjustable steering wheel. The idea had been prevalent for several years, but the Marr adaption was one of the more popular.

The Marr could be running and driven with the steering wheel in any of the positions. A change of wheel position was made without halting the movement of the car.

Powered by a 6½ h.p., one cylinder engine, the chain driven Marr was a product of the Marr Auto-Car Co. of Detroit, Mich. Actual manufacture was by the Fauber Company of Elgin, Ill.

1904 Marr

A baby automobile for two
by an aircraft company!

1929 MARTIN

A baby automobile — with a sixty-inch wheelbase and a total weight of six hundred pounds came on the scene in the "crash" year of 1929. This was an attempt to give the American motorist the last word in economical transportation. Overall size was approximately one-half of a normal size car.

The "Baby Martin" was designed by James V. Martin, and manufactured by the Martin Aeroplane Co. of Garden City, N. Y. The reputation of Mr. Martin in aircraft circles accounts for many of the aircraft features used on the car.

The body and frame were of integral construction. Each wheel made use of aviation cord as part of the individual wheel suspension. The cord withstood 25,000 miles of driving wear, and was easily replaced for a cost of eighty cents.

Individual drive shafts serving each rear wheel, was a feature made necessary by the use of separate wheel suspension. There were no axles, and the drive shafts were equipped with universal joints at the rear wheels.

In the front, the kingpins were made extra long, and the knuckles slid up and down on them. This is a trait of a landing gear on an airplane. Mr. Martin was partially responsible for the modern type of landing gear. A four cylinder air cooled engine supplied power for this unusual car.

Cars were shipped in weather proof packing cases with a hinged door. The purpose of this idea was to enable the car owner to use the case as a garage. The manufacturer contended that it was easy to push or pull the car in or out of the case.

For $250 the purchaser of the Martin received a two passenger car, a garage, and a claim of fifty miles of driving with a gallon of gas.

1929 Martin

The cyclecar craze was
an attempt at economy!

1914 MERCURY CYCLECAR

A true cyclecar — was a cheaper-to-buy-and-operate automobile. Economy was the by-word, and almost anything could be repaired with a screw driver and small wrench. Fifty miles with a gallon of gasoline made this car a champion among the economy minded drivers.

Some companies that produced cyclecars were reluctant to call them as such. Not so with the Mercury Cyclecars Co. of Detroit, Mich. They were proud of their car, and the venture proved to be one of the more successful.

A true cycle car had a two cylinder engine, tandem seats, belt drive, narrow tread, friction drive, transmission and bicycle type wheels. The Mercury utilized a two cylinder air cooled engine and friction drive. Eliminated from the Mercury were a frame, differential and gears.

The two passenger touring delivered for $375. Other models available were a one passenger roadster and a delivery van.

1914 Mercury Cyclecars.

All was optional except wheels and gearshift!

1919 MEYER

An optional car — for the buyer who wanted something different. Options ranged from two- to twelve-cylinder engines, and two- to nine-passenger models. Only compulsory components were the Meyer wheels and the specially designed gearshift.

The wheels were made of pressed steel and welded to the shell of the hub. Inside the hub shell were the collar and bearings. Between the hub shell and bearing collar was an unusual construction of rubber wedges.

With a pneumatic-tired wheel there is a tendency to iron out road bumps, and together with springs, most of the blows are smoothed to a gentle up and down movement. In the Meyer wheel, the rubber wedges in the hub were so constructed and placed that they could be forced in a longitudinal direction only. The springs and tires absorbed the remaining road shock.

The tires were not pneumatics, but hollow rubber in construction. Two hollow sections supported by a center wall and casing made the tire flexible. There was a groove directly above the supporting center wall, forming two running surfaces.

Shifting gears was made a fine art. Everything was as it should have been until the car was brought to a stop. At this point the transmission automatically was set in starting speed, and the clutch disengaged. Upon release of the emergency brake the car would move ahead in low gear. By pressing a small foot lever the car would be in running speed, or in any gear desired.

In going from high to reverse, disengaging the clutch auto-matically engaged the gears. The small foot lever could be pressed, shifting the gears automatically through first and allowing the reverse gear to be engaged, even though the car was in forward motion. According to the company no harm could be done.

This $6,500 car was manufactured by the A. J. Meyer Corp. of Chicago, Ill.

1919 Meyer

A retractable top on a
fabulous 325 h.p. car!

1930 MILLER SPECIAL

A retractable convertible top — on this car
that was capable of 135 m.p.h. speed. It was absolutely essential to either remove the canvas top,
or make an arrangement to have it protected from
tearing, caused by wind currents at high speed.
Harry A. Miller engineered this high performance
car with the look-to-the-future top.

The Miller Special was not the first to use the retractable top idea. Manufacture of the Miller Special was in the J. Gerard Kirchoff Body Works in Pasadena, Calif. To have the clean, sleek body lines that the speed of the car demanded, something had to be done with the canvas top and boot that went with it.

This was accomplished by having the entire top retract into the rear deck of the car. To raise the deck lid, it was necessary to pull the back of the seat forward, and crank a small handle. This handle operated an arrangement that locked the deck lid at three separate points when the deck was closed.

With the seat pulled forward no one could drive the car. Consequently there was no chance of the top being torn to shreds or the rear deck lid being ripped off. To lessen the rippling of the canvas, (common to soft tops at high speed driving), the leading portion of the top was made of metal, and fit flush with the windshield.

All the special features of the top, and its storage in the car, were brought about by the fact that the 325 h.p. engine enabled this car to attain speeds to 135 m.p.h. The extra radiator cap was for the super-charger cooling unit. The super-charger operated at 36,000 revolutions per minute.

1930 Miller Special

151

The tilt body for easy access to engine and components!

1905 MODEL

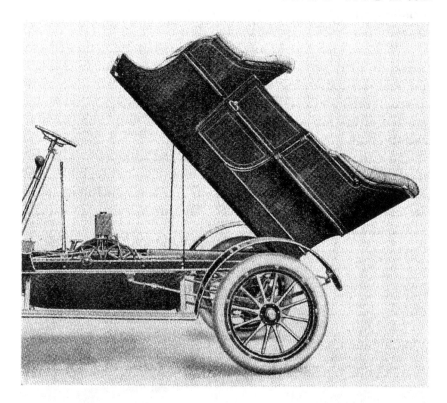

Raise the body — don't get out and get under! A hinged rear tonneau enabled the driver to have easy access to the engine, transmission and differential of this "model" automobile. The tilt body is still in use today on modern trucks — something "new" taken from 1905?

Accessibility to components of an automobile was the goal of the Model Automobile Co. of Peru, Ind. They were advocates of placing the engine in the middle of the car to eliminate vibration and induce a smoother ride.

This prompted the creation of the tilt body, since engine adjustment and repair was a perplexing matter, when located in the mid-section.

The body was hinged at the rear to the back frame piece. One man could raise the entire tonneau and hold it upright by placing the brace rods in position. Once this was accomplished the entire undercarriage, as well as engine, transmission and differential, were easy to service.

The idea was a good one—so good in fact that it is employed today on some trucks. They don't build them like they used to; or do they?

1905 Model

Self-adjusting air clutch and air brakes were real!

1907 NORTHERN

Air clutch and air brakes — two features not to be found on other cars of 1907, made the Northern an unusual car. The car of many "firsts" was built under the patents and guidance of Charles B. King.

The air compressor unit in the car created sixty pounds pressure for the air brakes. The brakes were applied by moving the brake lever — the amount of lever movement determined the braking power. A conventional locking ratchet brake was used for an emergency.

Operation of the air clutch was slightly more technical, but equally as easy for the driver to operate. To make it work, just turn the grip under the steering wheel a quarter of a turn. To release, turn it back to the original position. When the grip was turned, a port was opened in the forward end of the hollow crank shaft. Compressed air was admitted to an air pocket between the flywheel wall and a large leather disc.

The disc would expand slightly, clamping a metal disc, which in direct connection with the universal joint and drive shaft, formed the rear axle drive. There was absolutely no jerk that was common with the conventional type clutches used in other cars. The clutch would release instantly when the air pressure was cut off. The normal clutch pressure of sixty pounds per square inch would total 19,440 pounds. In times of stress, the pressure could be raised to 150 pounds per square inch, resulting in an unheard of 48,600 pounds of pressure on the clutch.

Another specialty of the Northern was the starting lever. This was not a crank in the true sense of the word, since the operator did not have to stoop. The lever handle was always in an upright position, and the engine was started by pulling the lever from right to left. A connection between the starting lever and the commutator made it impossible to advance the spark while the car was being started. Therefore, the kick-back was eliminated.

The Northern claimed to be the first car to have: three point engine support; entire mechanism enclosed in a combined gear and crank case; large fan and flywheel cast integral; only one universal joint between flywheel and rear axle; no truss or strut rods; side running boards; and all mechanism placed under the hood instead of under the floor of the car.

This car from Detroit, Mich. was one of the first to have fender mounted headlights. Without a top, the manufacturer sold their runabout for $3,500.

An underslung, inverted frame was a style rage!

1914 NORWALK

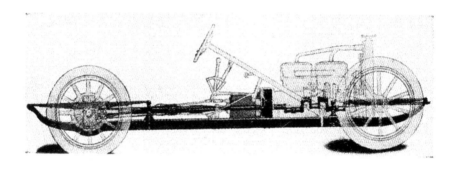

Underslung — the most romantic and descriptive word used in the early teens to describe a car's construction and style. The prominent idea behind underslung frame positioning was to permit a lower center of gravity, and reduce chances of turn over. A secondary, but nevertheless important result, was styling beauty. None were more sleek, racy or exciting to look at than the underslung models that appeared in the third decade of automobile manufacturing.

The Norwalk Motor Car Co. of Martinsburg, W. Va. was not the first to use the underslung style of construction, but they did bring the form to a high degree of perfection. The idea behind underslung construction was to get the car closer to the road. This was accomplished by placing the frame in an inverted position. In most cars the frame is positioned over the axles and the spring horns turn down in front and rear.

On the underslung, the frame members passed under the axles, and as the horns came from under the body, they turned up. This then necessitated a different type of suspension. Leaf springs were used, but they were completely flat and placed upside down in the shackles. As weight was placed on the car the springs were pulled down. When hitting a bump the springs were pushed upward to absorb the shock. The center of gravity, the center of suspension, and the center support all came to one level—a point even with the springs.

Side-sway, bouncing and skidding were greatly controlled and the possibility of turning over was practically non-existent. Most underslung models had larger wheels than used on other cars. This created a fender line even with hood line — a sleek, low silhouette.

1914 Norwalk

An American sports car
with laminated body!

1917 NOVARA

An American sports car — for the hell-bent-for-leather driving set, who found a half-way smooth road on any given week end. Boat tail, wire wheels and laminated mahogany body, with a guaranteed speed of 80 m.p.h., were all calculated to give the gay blade of 1917 a feeling of individuality and distinction as he piloted the Novara.

The dynamic Novara of Bristol, R. I. was produced in lots of twenty-five by the Herreshoff Manufacturing Co., noted for their building of yachts and power boats for pleasure. This explains the beautiful craftsmanship in the laminated mahogany body. Laminations were riveted with copper, and the interior was lined with cedar.

The frame was made of special alloy steel, one-tenth of an inch thick, and shaped to fit the body. Usual spring connections were used on the front, but in back the frame came to a point with the rear body section upswept.

Spare wheel and tire were carried under the turned up rear section, and the protruding spare tire served as a bumper. Cycle fenders and bullet headlamps, topped off by staggered seats, added the purist flair to this natty sportster that was introduced three months before United States entry into World War I.

Fifty miles per hour in second, eighty in high — these were the after-effects of a powerful engine and a total car weight of 1,500 pounds. There was still time to spend $2,750 for a Novara before joining the doughboys over there in 1917.

1917 Novara

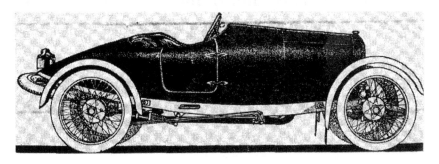

Eight-wheel cars were an idea for smooth riding!

1912 OCTOAUTO

Eight wheels and tires — designed to provide a luxury ride, and to the contrary of public opinion, increase tire mileage. M. O. Reeves' idea was not a passing fancy, but a sincere attempt to offer something creative to the automobile industry. Less tire wear was a welcome result for the already tire poor motorist of 1912.

Basically the Octoauto was a 1911, Model 53, Overland with alterations made at the Reeves Pulley Co. in Columbus, Ind. The original wheelbase was shortened to start with, but the final overall length following the addition of extra wheels was a whopping 175 inches.

All original components were left intact, and in place of the front and rear axles, Reeves used two cross shafts. At each end of the shafts a pivot box was located with 36 inch springs attached. This meant that there actually were eight sets of leaf springs on the car.

Springs were aligned with the body, but at the same time were allowed tolerance for a rocking motion. A regular axle was attached to each end of the springs. The two front axles and the extreme rear axle were identical and were used for steering.

The first rear axle was the power source, and the car pivoted on the attached wheels when turning. The steering shaft ran the entire length of the undercarriage. When negotiating a corner the two sets of front wheels turned in the same direction, while the rear wheels turned in an opposite course. The turning radius was quite short as compared to the lengthy wheelbase.

Reeves claimed eight tires on one car would out wear two sets of four. His reasoning pointed out that car weight was supported by eight wheels, and that harsh road shock was minimized by the car being nearly level at all times. When one wheel was in a hole or rut the wheel immediately behind was on level ground, and therefore tire strain was limited. This principle held true for the riding quality of the car.

Mr. Reeves intended to market this car and made an appeal for dealers in the trade journals of the day.

1912 Octoauto

161

One cylinder engine powered

this car up to 60 m.p.h.!

1911 ONLY

One, 60, 30 — this combination of numbers very capably describes the statistics for the Only. Amazing speed for a one cylinder engine that squeezed 30 miles of driving from a gallon of gasoline. To make it more unusual, the driver sat over the rear axle. Long on hood, short on passenger and luggage space, this car was so fantastic it had to be remembered!

The idea and design were from the Only Car Co. of Port Jefferson, N. Y. When automobiles first became popular, most of them were powered by one cylinder engines. By 1906 these were giving way to more cylinders, and by 1911 there were many sixes on the road.

When the Only was first shown at the New York Auto Show, imagine the astonishment of the viewers when they raised the hood, and saw the vertical one cylinder engine mounted up front by the radiator. The tremendous power was created by the ten inch stroke with a proportionately large bore of five and one-eighth inches. To add to the uniqueness, there were double flywheels enclosed in the crankcase.

With this arrangement the driver was sitting over the rear axle. Passenger and luggage space were at an absolute minimum. Undoubtedly the designer believed in the saying "it's what's up front that counts."

The unheard of Only was entered in a hill climbing event by the company as a promotion idea. Before the day was over the name Only was on everyone's lips. The single cylinder, 12 h.p. demon had won over all comers up to the six cylinder, 60 h.p. Palmer-Singer. The lone unbeatable entry was the 200 h.p. Fiat.

The Only was guaranteed to go 60 m.p.h.; travel 30 miles on a gallon of gasoline; and by written contract was guaranteed for one year, with free repair. What more could the driver sitting over the rear axle in front of the gasoline tank want for $800?

1911 Only

163

A compact car that proved popular the world over!

1903 ORIENT BUCKBOARD

A compact car — this one the ancestor of all compacts, and a very useful and desirable runabout. There were times when this car outsold every other car offered to the public. It was said the sun never sets on the Orient Buckboard since it was in use around the world.

Originally this little car, built by the Waltham Manufacturing Co. in Waltham, Mass. was an only product. Their original idea was to build a car that everyone could drive anywhere. Some of the first patents were issued in the early months of 1903.

At the beginning it was a two passenger runabout as shown in the first illustration. Just as the name implies it was a buckboard with the frame close to the ground, and a trifle sway back under a load. A rear-mounted one cylinder engine supplied the power. There was no body work, hood or tonneau; just the wood frame and floor with mounted seat. Steering was by tiller and there was only one speed forward.

The initial price of the two passenger buckboard was $375. Within a year a four passenger surrey was on sale for $450. All new models were equipped with a two speed transmission and a well braced floor. Twenty miles per hour speeds were possible and hill climbing power was increased.

By 1905 two more models were available — the runabout and the tonneau. Both had front bonnets and some semblance of body work. They were equipped with steering wheels, but the little four horsepower engine was still in the rear without a cover.

In 1906 the buckboard was introduced with a friction drive. The company boasted thirty-five miles to a gallon of gasoline.

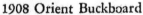

1908 Orient Buckboard

Folding seats converted

easily into a car bed!

1918 PAN

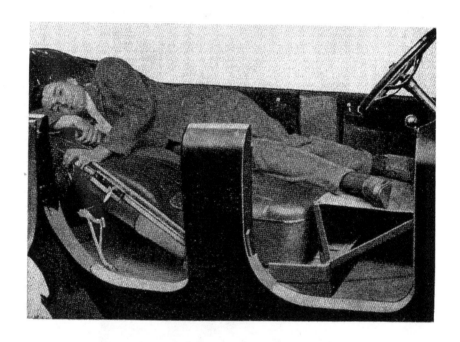

Folding seats — that converted into a bed for the driver of a Pan. No more wondering where you were going to sleep while traveling along the accommodation-scarce roads of 1917. Five simple steps were all that were needed to transform the seats into a bed for relaxing as snug as a bug in a Pan.

S. C. Pandolfo must have been an advocate of comfort and convenience in a motor car. He attempted to put his ideas to use by building the Pan in Saint Cloud, Minn. Reclining seats were one of the notable achievements that endeared the car to its owners.

Five seat-to-bed conversion steps as described in the owners manual were as follows:

1. Place gear shift lever in reverse position and set emergency brake lever forward as far as possible. 2. Remove cushion from rear seat and fold back board, then replace rear cushion. (The seat board made a stand for the cushion to rest on.) 3. Unlatch back of front seat by raising the two levers that hold it in position and swing backwards fitting the foot rail (on the tonneau floor) into brackets of the robe rail. 4. Remove the front cushion and fold out the fabric foot support. Then replace the front cushion so as to fill in the space at the bottom edge of the front seat and the fabric foot support. 5. Parts can be quickly replaced in proper positions for driving. Be sure in replacing, that the back of the front seat is securely locked in place. — IMPORTANT!

Buy stock in the company for $10 per share with a par value of $5. It was worth fifteen per cent discount on the price of a new $1,250 Pan car or other machines manufactured at Pan-Town-On-The Mississippi, alias Saint Cloud, Minn.

1918 Pan

No axles on this car with a plywood frame and body!

1921 PARENTI

No axles — on a car that was advertised as "the easiest riding car of all." Use of plywood paneling for the frame and body, resulted in an exceptionally strong unit weighing less than three hundred pounds. To lure people to consider buying such an unusual, and yet ordinary looking car, the manufacturer painted the first models bright orange.

Axles were done away with by the use of two transverse springs in front, and three in the rear of the car. They extended across the width of the car from wheel hanger to wheel hanger. Wheel alignment was maintained by pressed steel tie rods, which compelled them to rise and fall vertically when traveling over rough roads.

Since springs have a tendency to lengthen when they flatten out, the outer ends of the transverse springs were coiled around eccentric bronze bushings in the wheel hangers. As the wheels would rise when moving over a bump the bushings were forced to turn. This prevented the wheels from spreading, and the springs from cramping. In this way the springs became "axles." In the rear of the car the springs were placed in a triangular pattern, with one on top and two on the bottom. The top spring went into action only on overload or on extremely rough roads.

The frame and body were constructed of plywood paneling. The frame was of five-ply panels, twelve inches wide and three quarters of an inch thick, running the length of the chassis. Cross members of five-ply extended across the body, and were joined with pairs of pillars on both sides. The inside of the skeleton framework was three-ply panels. These were glued and screwed, resulting in an exceptionally sound body.

The Parenti, manufactured in Buffalo, N. Y., sported an eight cylinder air cooled engine and sold for $2,000.

1921 Parenti

169

Pneumatic suspension
for riding comfort!

1915 PNEUMOBILE

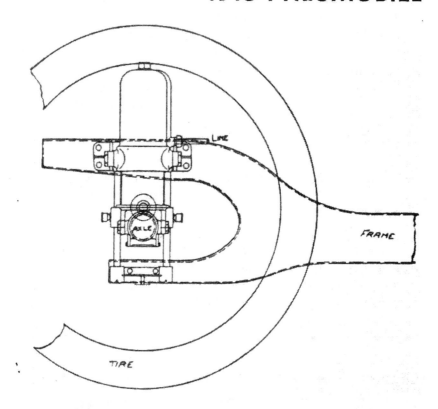

Pneumatic suspension — was one of the season's novelties for 1915. Success of a company was dependent on the public acceptance of this new idea. This system was to do away with suspension problems, but instead it did away with a company in one year. They dared be different, and lost.

After nine years of development the Cowles-MacDowell Co. of Chicago, Ill. introduced the Pneumobile with true pneumatic suspension. This is not to be confused with an air suspension system, since there is a definite difference. The air method usually relies on conventional springs to some degree.

Pneumobile featured a system of four cylinders mounted on the frame; one next to each wheel. They were co-acting with plungers rigidly supported by the axles without a metallic connection between the wheel, axle assembly and frame. For pressure equalizing purposes, the cylinders were connected by a central piping system. If one wheel was to hit a severe bump, the pressure would be lessened in that wheel, and increased in the other three, in order to keep the car on an even keel.

To accommodate the cylinders, a conventional frame was used, with the exception of the ends. Vertical forks were attached at the frame extremities to hold the cylinders rigid.

Company publicity stated that shock absorbtion was so great that solid tires could be used with as much resulting riding comfort as if pneumatic tires had been used. The Cowles-MacDowell idea did away with troublesome springs, shackles, hangers and heavy U-bolt assemblies, with an obvious reduction in total car weight. Other company-claimed benefits were: lower center of gravity, greater traction, ease of handling and elimination of torsional strain on frame and body.

A noticeable style change was the placing of the radiator filler cap under the hood — a first for the industry?

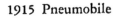

1915 Pneumobile

A car with cast aluminum
body, aluminum wheels!

1926 POMEROY

Aluminum sections — of the new Pomeroy body were cast in one piece, with the belt moulding formed at the same time. The rear of the body was unique, due to the fact that it was exceptionally wide. To keep in style and to give the body a narrow appearance, "horseshoe" moulding lines were used. Lower body quarters were cut out to form a concave effect, to eliminate the fullness of the rounded top corners.

Prior to the advent of the Pomeroy cast aluminum body, there had always been complications connected with the use of this metal. Body sections in earlier aluminum efforts were bolted together, with mouldings used to cover the joints. Sections were then placed over the wood framework.

Concave aluminum wheels with brake drums cast intregal were part of the standard equipment. Windshield posts were trimmed to a minimum to provide greated driver visibility. Door hinges also were cast of an aluminum alloy.

The Pomeroy was manufactured for the Aluminum Company of America in plants at Buffalo, N. Y. Two executives of the company designed the car. John S. Burdick created the body style, and L. H. Pomeroy designed the running gear and engine. At least seven of these cars were manufactured in three or four body styles.

1926 Pomeroy

An electric push button shift to select gears!

1917 PREMIER

Push button shift — by Cutler-Hammer, was an ingenious device that struck the public's fancy when it appeared on the Premier. Sales competition was keen, and the push button shift was calculated to create a new margin of superiority for the car from Indianapolis, Ind.

Automatic shifts have come and gone, dating from at least 1904. The use of the Cutler-Hammer shift on the Premier was a successful effort on the part of two great manufacturers to offer their product to the car buyers.

The original installation was an almost haphazard affair with a four push button box attached to the steering column. This unit was refined to the style shown in the illustration. The shift was completely electrical, and merely by pushing the buttons you selected the desired gear. Actual shifting took place when the clutch pedal was depressed.

Another feature of note on this car was the folding steering wheel. This was another version of how a stout man could enter and exit from a car with considerable ease.

A four passenger Premier roadster had a selling price of $1,685.

1917 Premier

175

Throttle wheel speed control

was convenient and easy!

1905 RAMBLER

Throttle wheel control — simplified driver acceleration efforts, and did away with many levers and gadgets. Traveling speed was controlled by the operator without removing a hand from the steering wheel. No excuse for one hand driving in this car!

The Thomas B. Jeffery Co. of Kenosha, Wisc. marketed their 1905 Rambler with the throttle wheel control. First impressions were that of a car with two steering wheels. The innovation proved successful, and was used and publicized for several years.

It was a simple matter for the driver to regulate traveling speed by merely gripping the throttle wheel with his fingers. Tilting the throttle wheel would increase or decrease speed as desired. Every speed, from the lowest to the highest, was possible without removing the hands from the steering wheel.

This then was one of the earliest attempts to offer operating convenience to the driver as well as helping keep his mind on driving. The Type One Surrey Rambler was priced at $1,350.

1905 Rambler

The colonial style car body
was a new idea in 1913!

1913 REGAL

Colonial styling — a closed car body construction approach that made possible the picturesque colonial coupes. The window arrangement and roof lines were reminiscent of the old colonial horse drawn coaches.

One of the smaller and better looking of all the colonial styled coupes offered by many manufacturers was the 1913 Regal. This underslung, $1,250 model was a product of the Regal Motor Car Co. of Detroit, Mich.

The window style served no apparent purpose other than for appearances. Solid body construction was highlighted by the double arch; an arch from front to rear, and side to side.

Closed cars were not common in 1913 so the colonial coupes made quite a hit with style and weather conscious motorists.

1913 Regal

An in-line three cylinder vibrationless engine!

1904 RELAY

An in-line three cylinder engine — was the main topic of conversation for addicts of the 1904 Relay. Not to be outdone by anyone in the engine department, this car's power plant developed 24 h.p., and gave vibrationless performance.

The Relay Motor Car Co. of Reading, Pa. manufactured this car that looked much like any other car of 1904, but when the hood was raised the resemblance ceased. The engine was an in-line three cylinder unit with the three cranks set at an angle of 120 degrees on the crankshaft. Both the inlet and exhaust valves were in the head on top of the cylinder.

The engine also featured seamless, brass tube, detachable water jackets. It wasn't uncommon for an auto owner in 1904 to put his car up on jacks for the winter. One of the usual ailments of a car stored for winter was frozen water systems. On the Relay all one had to do was to remove the water jackets, and all fear of freezing was eliminated. In the event that a water jacket was damaged by freezing it was cheaper to replace a jacket rather than the entire cylinder.

The engine hood was so constructed with hinges and spring catches that it could be opened from either side, or taken off completely. The gearshift was on the steering column directly under the steering wheel. The steering wheel itself could be tilted for easy entrance and exit. With all the above features, plus laminated wood fenders, the Relay sold for $2,000.

1904 Relay

Built-in trunks were rare until the RiChard debut!

1915 RiCHARD

Built-in trunks — a perfect solution to the problem of keeping luggage, spare tire, and folded top clean and dry. This sneak preview of a style trend to come in the thirties, was a drastic departure from the ordinary in 1915.

Before integration of the trunk into the automobile body it was an accessory. Trunks were available in beautifully finished woods, or enamelled to match the car's paint. Some trunks were specially built rounded models, that fit into the center of a flat mounted spare tire. Still others had custom made luggage pieces to fit the trunk interior.

In 1915 there was a remarkable departure from all these practices when the RiChard Manufacturing Co. of Cleveland, O. presented their car with built-in trunk.

The illustration shows in ghost the placement of luggage, spare tires and folded top in the closed trunk. The overhang which looks quite large, was said to be no greater than an ordinary touring with the top down, and two spare tires on back.

1915 RiChard

Steering was enjoyable

with right angle hubs!

1911 ROYAL TOURIST

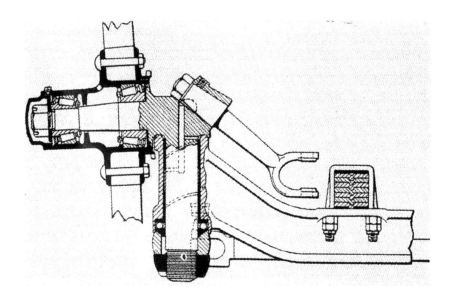

Easy steering — a boon to the driver who had to struggle with the mud, ruts and unpaved roads of the early 1900's. You could tour like royalty when you drove a Royal Tourist, if you had $4,800 extra dollars!

The Royal Tourist, manufactured by the Royal Tourist Motor Car Co. in Cleveland, O., was renowned for quality construction and advanced ideas, one of which was the right angle hub.

Instead of having the wheel spindle come out in a line with the solid front axle, a right angle hub was used. The vertical part of the hub fit into the axle and the horizontal hub protruded out and above at right angles to the vertical hub. The assembly was easily replaced by simply removing the nut on the lower end of the vertical hub and pulling it through the top of the axle.

The tie rod connected on the bottom, and the arm on top connected with the drag link to the radius arm of the steering gear. This was a well-balanced arrangement which made for one of the easiest steering cars of the day.

Style-wise the 1911 model was far advanced. While most other manufacturers continued to use the straight-line body and fender styling, the Royal Tourist stood out with full shell fenders and boat-type touring body. Remove the brass lights and alter the radiator design, and the style shown below could easily be placed in the year 1917.

1911 Royal Tourist

Collapsible windows on this car pre-dated hardtops!

1923 RUBAY

Collapsible windows — transformed this cabriolet from a closed to an open car in less than a minute. Rubay of Cleveland O., were creators of some of America's finest automobile coachwork. The car bearing their name was a fine example of pride of craftsmanship.

Side windows were divided into five equal parts, and joined together with piano hinges. A narrow metal sash held the windows in the correct position. Center windows were attached permanently to the car body by hinges on the bottom side.

To convert the car to an open model in less than a minute, the driver merely folded the windows from the front and back of the car, toward the center. After the windows were stacked in the center of the window area, a panel between the two doors folded down, and the windows were lowered into the body.

The cabriolet body on the 1923 Rubay was of French origin under the name of Baehr. Leon Rubay licensed the patent for use in the United States. The Rubay was a custom car with a corresponding price of $5,250.

Several other engineering advances were featured on the Rubay which helped to raise the selling price. Brake drums were of cast aluminum with steel linings cast into them. Brake shoes were also aluminum, and operated against the steel lining of the drum.

Half elliptic springs were used in front and back. The rear end of the front springs, and the front end of the rear springs, were fit into the usual type shackles. The opposite ends of the springs were rolled out flat, and passed between two hardened steel rollers. These ends were encased in the spring brackets and grease fittings attached. Innovations such as these seem to justify the price.

1923 Rubay

The car that featured a body of rainbow stripes!

1930 RUXTON

Rainbow-hued color bands — wide, in socko colors from roof line to exposed frame member, burst forth like a Fourth of July spectacular from the Ruxton shops in 1930 to cheer the depressed, broke, and daring motor car buyer. A choice of colors was offered. The hues graded from light and bright downward to dark and rich. The rainbow bands were 4 to 8 inches wide.

The design was a brainchild of Josef Urban, a highly respected designer of the day. It was low, only 62 inches high, and was breathtaking wherever seen.

There was more than eye-drenching delight. There was a superiority of drive, ride, and roadability performance contributed by its front wheel drive. The ride was like that found in an airplane. You sat low, and rode close to the ground.

The mechanical design was that of William J. Muller, who was a former member of the Edward G. Budd organization. Manufacture was by the Moon Co., St. Louis, Mo. Prices as expected — high, up to $4,600.

Many well known body builders adopted the Ruxton idea and turned out some of the most beautiful creations that have ever been put on wheels.

1930 Ruxton Front Wheel Drive

Built to order car with

many industry firsts!

1935 SCARAB

Built to order cars — with demonstrations by invitation only, was the policy of the Stout Motor Corp. of Dearborn, Mich. The word scarab is the name of a beetle regarded by people of ancient times as a symbol of creation or creative power. The Scarab car was a material example of creative power as interpreted by William B. Stout.

If design alone was not enough to make this car outstanding, then some of the firsts and innovations would rightly put it in that category. In some instances "they do build cars like they used to" in respect to features offered on the Scarab for 1935.

Examples of modern day applications of features previewed by the Scarab are: full unit body with no chassis, engine placed in rear, flush type door hinges, running boards as usable inside space, forced draftless ventilation, slanted windows to eliminate reflection and smooth unbroken body panels.

Other uncommon features found on the Scarab were: thermostatically controlled inside temperature, complete insulation against sound and temperature, electric door controls with no projecting handles, and no overhang with exceptionally long wheelbase.

Except for the driver's seat, all seats were loose and adjustable to any position. Card tables could be used inside the car, and the bench type seat converted to a full length couch. The Scarab in all its glory cost $5,000.

1935 Scarab

If the road ended abruptly
this car could be carried!

1921 SCOOTAMOBILE

Limited in size to be sure — but not to the point of being a toy. Just an uncomplicated two passenger, three wheel car that delivered 60 to 70 miles of driving with a gallon of gasoline. Space for transporting luggage or other merchandise was at a premium.

The Scootamobile was the brain child of C. H. Martin who was associated with the Rocking Fifth Wheel Co. of Springfield, Mass. before he organized the Martin Motor Co. in the same city.

A rear-mounted two cyclinder engine and transmission combination, with three forward and one reverse gear, plus extreme light weight, made the name prefix "scoot" an absolute truth. Weighing only one hundred and fifty pounds, the Scootamobile could actually be carried by two people.

Passengers were seated over the rear axle, and with the engine in the rear there was little danger of the car tipping over on its nose. The small triangular box frame made the car sturdy with good roadability. Steering was done with a lever type steering handle. For only $250 the economy minded driver could own a Scootamobile.

1921 Scootamobile

Two pistons for one cylinder eliminated engine vibrations!

1903 SHELBY

Two pistons and one cylinder — an automotive engineering fete that was officially titled a "three wrist, double throw" type engine. A major concern of car builders was engine vibration. The Shelby design was to be the answer to this problem.

The Shelby patent called for one large open-end cylinder fitted with two pistons. The engine shaft was actuated by both pistons. Number one piston was directly connected to the center wrist pin by the pitman. Having an elongated shaft, the other piston connected from the extreme end, and attached to the two connecting rods extending forward on either side of the cylinder. These engaged the two outer opposed wrists of the engine shaft.

The explosion took place between the heads of the pistons in this big cylinder, and the pistons travelled outward. Energy produced by such an engine was utilized to the fullest extent. There was no recoil effect, as with the common single cylinder engine.

It was said that the 1903 Shelby was a smooth and efficient car. The equal action of the two pistons, both moving at the same time, had a cushioning effect, and vibrations were practically eliminated.

Besides its unique engine, this car from the Shelby Motor Car Co. of Shelby, O. featured a front radiator and a telescoping steering column. The steering wheel could be raised or lowered to accommodate any size driver.

1903 Shelby

An automatic transmission utilized centrifugal force!

1907 STURTEVANT

Automatic transmissions — the mechanical answer to the phrase, "giddy ap." Utter not a sound, and you were on your way, just press on the Sturtevant driving button! The harder you pressed, the faster you moved. Here was a natural for the lead footed driver of 1907.

The 1907 Sturtevant automatic transmission was an improved version of the 1904 model introduced by the Sturtevant Mill Co. of Boston, Mass. Centrifugal force was the key to the entire patent.

Two clutches were enclosed in an oil-tight, hollow flywheel. These components appeared on other cars of the period, but the Sturtevant was the first to have them all in one car.

The driving button, as they called it, was located on the inclined floor board. As you pressed down on the button the engine shaft started turning. When the shaft and low speed clutch turned fast enough, weights on the outer rims of the clutch would move out, engaging the clutch to drive the car forward. The more you pressed the faster the shaft would turn, and the more positive the clutch became engaged.

When the low speed clutch capacity was reached, the high speed clutch would "kick in," leaving the low speed mechanism to turn freely on the shaft. This worked conversely in slowing down or negotiating a steep hill. As the engine revolutions decreased the weights moved toward the center of the shaft. Consequently the high speed and low speed clutches were disengaged.

The engine idled at 220 rpm's, which was too few to cause movement of the centrifugal weights. A full governor control was in effect during idling. An automatic button brake, as described by the company, would lock automatically if the car made any movement while idling. This was an important and necessary safety feature!

The flying roadster for $3,500 used an early version of the popular rumble seat. The company described the seat in this manner, "there was also a concealed rear seat that could be discovered on occasion."

Did this mean the seat was hard to find or difficult to open?

Safety glass to protect people in car accidents!

1926 STUTZ

Safety glass — specifically named "Protex" was used to highlight safety features of the 1926 Stutz. A special measure of breaking resistance was incorporated into the windshield by imbedding fine strands of wire in the glass. Larger, faster and more cars, coupled with increased total miles of driving, spurred the accident rate in the twenties. Large numbers of fatalities and serious injuries were directly accountable to shattered and flying glass.

Recognizing the urgent need for greater driver and passenger protection from the hazards of broken glass injuries, the Stutz Motor Car Co. of Indianapolis, Ind. budgeted over a quarter of a million dollars for use of safety glass in all their car windows. The ventilating window eaves on the sedans were also made of safety glass.

An unusual item of car ownership protection provided by the Stutz company was the use of the Fedco System which was under the William J. Burns Detective Agency. A number plate was affixed to the dash of each car in such a way that it could not be removed without mutilation. As a result the stolen Stutz was a rarity, and a valued protection service was assured the owner.

1926 Stutz

A three-wheel car that was

commercial sales success!

1913 WAGENHALLS

A three-wheel car — ever a point of conten-
tion for many of the formative years of the automobile industry. Such men as C. W. Kelsey and
C. E. Duryea were proponents of the tricycle running gear idea.

W. G. Wagenhalls of Detroit, Mich. produced the 1913 Wagenhalls which was perhaps the most perfected of all early three-wheel efforts. The commercial version of this car was manufactured in quantity for use by the United States post office department.

A four cylinder engine was rated at twenty horsepower and was mounted on a sub-frame. Engine replacement could be made in less than a half hour's time. Power transmission was by a chain to the rear wheel.

In the commercial model the driver sat more toward the back of the chassis. The forward area was taken up by the parcel carrying box. Both open and closed boxes were available with a load capacity of nearly a half ton.

Prices ranged from $690 to $1,100 for this eighty inch wheelbase car that weighed approximately one ton.

1913 Wagenhalls

Self-charging electric

car with great range!

1917 WOODS DUAL POWER

Dual power options — designed to put an end to the problem of time lost for battery recharging, and limited driving range associated with ordinary electric powered cars. Travel near or far was possible with the always ready electric motor or auxiliary gasoline engine!

The Woods Dual Power manufactured in Chicago, Ill. by the Woods Motor Vehicle Co. was basically an electric car. The small gasoline engine under the hood had a 2½x3½ bore, resulting in high r.p.m.'s, and limited power.

Starting for a trip was usually done with electric power. On the steering wheel were located two levers similar to spark and throttle quadrants. A meter on the dash indicated the amount of charge in the twenty-four cell battery. At the driver's feet was a pedal with a pad, that could be oscillated forward or backward.

In starting the driver could either move the outside lever as he would to apply more gas, or he released the foot pedal, and raised the same hand lever an inch or so. Removing his foot from the pedal the car would glide away silently under electric power. Acceleration was accomplished by pushing the hand lever upward. Top speed was approximately 20 m.p.h. During such driving, a meter on the dash indicated there was a full charge of electricity passing from the battery to the electric motor.

When the electric supply diminished the gasoline engine was started by moving the other hand lever slowly upward. There was a slight braking action and an electric clutch would engage the gasoline engine and start it. At this time the car was operating on both electric and gasoline power. Top speed was close to 35 m.p.h. While traveling this fast the amount of current being supplied the electric motor could be diminished. Excess electric current was directed into the battery. The dash meter indicated that such an operation was taking place at the same time power was being transmitted to drive the car.

The electric control lever could be fully retarded, and the car motivated by gasoline engine only. Under this circumstance the electric motor became a generator, and all of the power created was used in charging the battery.

An oddity of this car was the fact that in order to travel in reverse, the electric motor had to be engaged. This was accomplished by use of the foot pedal and oscillating the pad forward, and at the same time placing the heel of the shoe on a small lever against the heel board under the driver's seat. Bring the pedal backwards again and the car reversed. The pedal was actually the means of opening and closing the switch on the electric motor.

Picture Credits

The photographs used as illustrations in the book are hereby credited alphabetically to the collections from which they were obtained.

A. B. C., Stanley K. Yost Collection
Ackerman, Automobile Manufacturers Association
Alstel, Stanley K. Yost Collection
Atlas, Stanley K. Yost Collection
Atlas, engine, Automotive History Collection, Detroit Public Library
Autocycle, Stanley K. Yost Collection
Auto Red Bug, Automotive History Collection, Detroit Public Library
Bantam, Automobile Manufacturers Association
Barrows, Stanley K. Yost Collection
Barrows, phaeton, Automobile Manufacturers Association
Balzer, Stanley K. Yost Collection
Beverly, Stanley K. Yost Collection
Briscoe, Stanley K. Yost Collection
Brush, Automotive History Collection, Detroit Public Library
Cadillac, Automotive History Collection, Detroit Public Library
Caloric, Automobile Manufacturers Association
Cameron, Automobile Manufacturers Association
Carter, Automobile Manufacturers Association
Carter, chassis, Stanley K. Yost Collection
Cartercar, Manning Bros. Photographers, Highland Park, Mich.
Cartercar, friction drive, Stanley K. Yost Collection
Century Electric, Manning Bros. Photographers, Highland Park. Mich.
Century Electric, foot pedal, Stanley K. Yost Collection
Charter, Automotive History Collection, Detroit Public Library
Christie, Stanley K. Yost Collection
Christie, wheel, Automobile Manufacturers Association
Club Car, Stanley K. Yost Collection
Coleman, Stanley K. Yost Collection
Columbia-Knight, Stanley K. Yost Collection
Columbia Magnetic, Stanley K. Yost Collection
Columbia Six, Stanley K. Yost Collection
Coats Steam, Automotive History Collection, Detroit Public Library
Cotta, Stanley K. Yost Collection
Cotta, chassis, Automotive History Collection, Detroit Public Library
Cruiser, Stanley K. Yost Collection
Day Utility, car, Automobile Manufacturers Association
Day Utility, truck, Automotive History Collection, Detroit Public Library

Detroit Air Cooled, Stanley K. Yost Collection
Detroit Air Cooled, engine, Automotive History Collection, Detroit
    Public Library
Diana, Stanley K. Yost Collection
Direct Drive, Stanley K. Yost Collection
Drexel, Stanley K. Yost Collection
Duck, Stanley K. Yost Collection
Duquesne, Stanley K. Yost Collection
Duquesne, seat, Automotive History Collection, Detroit Public Library
Dyke, Automotive History Collection, Detroit Public Library
Eagle-Macomber, Automotive History Collection, Detroit Public Library
Flint, Automobile Manufacturers Association
Flint, chassis, Stanley K. Yost Collection
Frontmobile, Stanley K. Yost Collection
Gearless, Stanley K. Yost Collection
Glover, Automotive History Collection, Detroit Public Library
Graham, Stanley K. Yost Collection
Grout Steam, Stanley K. Yost Collection
Gyroscope, Automotive History Collection, Detroit Public Library
Hal Twelve, Stanley K. Yost Collection
Hamlin, Automotive History Collection, Detroit Public Library
Harrison, Automotive History Collection, Detroit Public Library
Harrison, engine, Stanley K. Yost Collection
Haynes-Apperson, Stanley K. Yost Collection
Haynes-Apperson, restored, Jack A. Frost, Washington, Mich.
Heine-Velox, Automotive History Collection, Detroit Public Library
Hewitt, Automotive History Collection, Detroit Public Library
Heyman, Stanley K. Yost Collection
Heyman, engine, Automotive History Collection, Detroit Public Library
Hub Electric, Stanley K. Yost Collection
Hub Electric, wheel hub, Automobile Manufacturers Association
Intrepid, Stanley K. Yost Collection
Ingram-Hatch, Automotive History Collection, Detroit Public Library
Jordan, Automobile Manufacturers Association
Jordan, Woodlite, Automotive History Collection, Detroit Public Library
King, Stanley K. Yost Collection
Kissel, 1916, E. E. Husting, Boston, Mass.
Kissel, 1917, Stanley K. Yost Collection
Kissel, 1920, (restored) E. E. Husting, Boston, Mass.
Lozier, Stanley K. Yost Collection
Lozier, differential, Automotive History Collection, Detroit Public Library
Lyons-Knight, Stanley K. Yost Collection
Majestic, Stanley K. Yost Collection
Marion, Stanley K. Yost Collection
Marmon, Stanley K. Yost Collection
Marr, Stanley K. Yost Collection
Mercury Cyclecar, Manning Bros. Photographers, Highland Park, Mich.
Martin, car, R. L. Porter, New York, N. Y.
Martin, cars, Automotive History Collection, Detroit Public Library
Meyer, Stanley K. Yost Collection
Miller Special, Stanley K. Yost Collection
Model, Automotive History Collection, Detroit Public Library
Northern, Automotive History Collection, Detroit Public Library
Norwalk, Automotive History Collection, Detroit Public Library
Novara, Automotive History Collection, Detroit Public Library
Novara, front, Stanley K. Yost Collection
Octoauto, Automotive History Collection, Detroit Public Library
Octoauto, front, Automobile Manufacturers Association

Only, Automotive History Collection. Detroit Public Library
Orient Buckboard, Stanley K. Yost Collection
Pan, Automotive History Collection. Detroit Public Library
Parenti, Automobile Manufacturers Association
Parenti, front. Stanley K. Yost Collection
Pneumobile, Stanley K. Yost Collection
Pomeroy. Stanley K. Yost Collection
Premier, Stanley K. Yost Collection
Premier, shift. Automotive History Collection, Detroit Public Library
Rambler. Stanley K. Yost Collection
Regal. Manning Bros. Photographers. Highland Park. Mich.
Relay. Automotive History Collection. Detroit Public Library
RiChard, Stanley K. Yost Collection
Royal Tourist. Stanley K. Yost Collection
Rubay, Stanley K. Yost Collection
Rubay, windows, Automotive History Collection. Detroit Public Library
Ruxton, Automobile Manufacturers Association
Scarab. Automobile Manufacturers Association
Scootamobile, Automobile Manufacturers Association
Scootamobile, chassis, Automotive History Collection. Detroit Public Library
Shelby, Automotive History Collection. Detroit Public Library
Sturtevant, Automotive History Collection. Detroit Public Library
Stutz, Manning Bros. Photographers. Highland Park, Mich.
Wagenhalls, Raymond Welke. Detroit, Mich.
Wagenhalls. chassis, Automotive History Collection. Detroit Public Library
Woods Dual Power, Automotive History Collection, Detroit Public Library

GENERAL MOTORS LIBRARIES

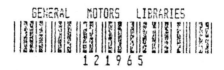

1 2 1 9 6 5

629.209   Y83

DSL   TL23 .Y88
1963
                              c. 1
                              121965

Yost, Stanley K

  They don't build cars like
  they used to!

DATE DUE

DEMCO 38-297

Printed in the USA
CPSIA information can be obtained
at www.ICGtesting.com
LVHW022023171123
764248LV00005B/506

9 781014 123183